Beowulf for Business:

The Warrior's Guide to Career Building

Beowulf for Business:

The Warrior's Guide to Career Building

E. L. Risden

Whitston Publishing Company, Inc.
Albany, New York
2007

Library of Congress Control Number 2006928989

ISBN 978-0-87875-566-0

Printed in the United States of America

Contents

Introduction

The Practical Poem for People
in Business
(And Other Professions)

Why You Should Read This Book

In the movie *Annie Hall*, Woody Allen's character, Alvie, suggests that before Annie signs up for any college course, she ought to consult him so that she doesn't have to read something like *Beowulf*.

What a shame if she doesn't read it.

What a shame if you don't read it, too.

It's packed with great advice.

I can imagine an unfilmed sequel in which Annie and Alvie read *Beowulf* together while they picnic in Central Park. Annie says that the poem begins with a funeral so that we remember that mortality catches up to all of us, even heroes. Alvie says that's silly: the funeral shows the poet's hypochondriacal tendencies and his debilitating obsession with his father. Annie calls to a passer-by, who happens to be the reincarnation of the author of *Beowulf*—he has learned of his past life from a Brooklyn medium recommended by Shirley MacLaine. He disgustedly tells Alvie that Annie is in fact right and that Alvie has once again projected himself onto everyone he meets and everything he reads. Annie thanks the poet and smiles triumphantly at Alvie, who, once the poet has gone on his way, harangues her for ten minutes about how, okay, maybe he was wrong: the poet was obsessed with his *mother* rather than his father or he wouldn't have taken the trouble to travel all the way to New York to endorse Annie's aggressive arguments.

We won't see that sequel released any time soon.

But it suggests another reason why you should read *Beowulf*: so that you experience the great work itself rather than relying on someone's interpretation. In this case I don't say so out of a belief that the classic literature of the past has an intrinsic power to make any thoughtful reader a better person—though I do believe that—but because *Beowulf* has powerful, immediate, practical applications that will help you get enormously better in whatever profession you choose to pursue.

In this book we will explore applications of the great Old English epic to business, but, Sun Tzu-like, you may implement what you learn according to your own needs and aspirations, regardless of your field of endeavor. *Beowulf* can help empower you to live a better, more successful life.

Yes, *better* and *successful* are complicated words, but I use them advisedly: I mean that if you study *Beowulf* even a bit, you can both become a better person and find more success in the working world, particularly in business.

Some books have that power. The great works of the world's

religions have it. Shakespeare's plays, novels by Dostoyevsky, Hugo, and Morrison, Dante's *Divine Comedy*, Milton's *Paradise Lost*, Barrett Browning's *Aurora Leigh*, Thoreau's *Walden*, Borges' short stories, any number of the greatest and great literary works of all time have it: the capability to change your life. And I'll bet your own favorite novels, plays, biographies, poems, and even self-help books have it, too—that's part of what has made them your favorites and in some cases the favorites of your parents, grandparents, and great-grandparents.

Please recall to mind those favorite books. Don't you feel proud that you read them, whether they're technical discussions of particle physics or internal combustion engines, graphic novels of intrigue and adventure, or children's stories? Don't you believe that knowing them has enriched your life, that by reading them you've become a smarter, stronger, more aware, more savvy person better able to deal with the day-to-day struggles of life? Your first answer may be, "Sorry, I still have trouble with the day-to-day struggles of life" or "Ha, I've learned from the School of Hard Knocks, not from books." But I suspect that no matter how much or little reading you've done, whether you read for knowledge or pure entertainment, without digging too deeply you'll recall a book that in some way has made your life better and continues to do so.

If you can't think of such a book, put down this one, ask some friends who read a lot to recommend the books they'd take with them to that proverbial desert island, read at least two or three of those they've especially praised, and then come back to *Beowulf for Business*. You'll feel glad you did it, and you'll be ready for everything I'll ask you to think about as we proceed together.

Some people say, "I don't like complex books, and I don't like to read too deeply into them. I just like to use a good book to get away from problems or to pass the time on the train to work."

For you I'll try to keep this book clear, readable, and to the point—if nothing else, the person reading over your shoulder on the train will think you an up-and-coming star in the business world since you read interesting books even on the train. You won't even need to confess that this one's easy.

For people who search for really complex books and love to devour them at all levels: if you haven't read it yet, you'll love *Beowulf* (yes, love it) when you do read it, and I'll prepare you to dig out as many layers, truths, and applicable tidbits as I can. What's more, if you read the poem later, on your own, particularly after we've worked together, you'll find many additional applications to suit your circumstances. *Beowulf* is that complex and that good. And more popular than you or Alvie might think: one scholar has observed that it's the most written-about book in the tradition of literature in English— more than *Hamlet*, *Paradise Lost*, or *Moby Dick*. If you have read *Beowulf*, you're ready to add to your understanding: you'll find ways to answer that hackneyed but persistent question, what can a book like that do for me?

And I want you to find this book eminently practical. If you use it as a guide, it will help you find in *Beowulf* doorways into the wisdom of the ancients, wisdom that has long survived its authors and that can and will help you and me accomplish a range of goals, anything from just getting up in the morning and surviving a day's work to climbing the corporate ladder to feeling, later in your career, that within the bounds of human possibility you have done your best to live a satisfying life.

Together you and *Beowulf* can do that. So let's get started.

About *Beowulf*

Beowulf is a great epic/heroic poem from the early Middle Ages. *Epic* means a long, heroic narrative poem that explores some question or virtue central to the people from whom it comes. Every year someone teaches *Beowulf* at nearly every high school and college in the English-speaking world. Written in a language we call Old English or sometimes Anglo-Saxon (a term better used to describe the culture from which it comes), the poem probably began as a recitation presented by a poet to an audience of upper-class warriors at a mead hall, a place where soldiers strengthened their bonds of community by eating, drinking, and talking together. It combines Christian elements with those of pagan Germanic culture.

We don't know who composed the poem or when the composer completed it. Scholars have proposed dates from the Seventh Century to the Eleventh Century. We do know it was recorded—only one copy survives—in the early years of the Eleventh Century in England. The mostly legible manuscript rests honorably in the British Library in London. You can see it there, protected under glass, one of the great treasures from the medieval world. You can get printed copies of it in Old English and even a facsimile edition. You'll have an easier time with the original if you can read some German, but if you really want to read it, you'll have to acquire some Old English through training and study.

But no worries: you can find many good translations (some better than others). Your local bookstore or library will probably have more than one, and a decent English teacher can advise you about which to try. Or if you'd like, write me through our mutual friend the publisher and I'll recommend what I like best and trust most. A translation is seldom a word-by-word rendering of the original text into your language because that method just doesn't work: every language has its unique word patterns, history, and range of feel and connotation. So you can read different translations and have quite different experiences of a book's ideas and its beauty. Yes, *Beowulf* has beauty, like that of good, clean hardwood or polished stone.

As epic poems go (compare the *Iliad* and the *Aeneid*, for instance), *Beowulf* is pretty short: only 3,182 lines, some hundred or so pages in print, about the length of a pre-Harry Potter children's novel or of a story in a condensed-novel series. Before anyone recorded *Beowulf*, the performers, called *scops*, may have spoken or chanted it in any number of versions, perhaps over the course of a two- or three-evening presentation—we have no way of knowing. Now you can read it comfortably in a couple evenings or a weekend. If you give it a go, you may find it slow at first—hey, it was written down a millennium ago!—but once you get comfortable with the rhythms, poetic patterns, and periodic digressions, *Beowulf* will rock you along as if you were sailing on a calm ocean. If you'd rather just read this book and avoid the original for now, I'll give you enough of the poem right here so that by the time we've finished, you'll feel as though it's an old friend, if not an exceedingly close one. At least you'll know what you can get from it that you can take to work with you on a daily basis, the part that will help you build a career.

You should know from the beginning of our work together that *Beowulf* is inherently a heroic, instructive, moral poem: the poet aimed not only to please, but also to teach lessons to the audience. Unlike modern authors, medieval ones believed teaching their audience something important was essential to their craft. Medievals wrote and read on multiple levels at once; for them, everything was potentially *allegorical*—that is, the main story referred to other parallel stories that taught about history or morality. They wanted to dig deep.

On the other hand, if you don't want to learn something, you don't pick up a book like that—but then you wouldn't be reading a book like this one, either. Neither you nor I need agree with anything in the poem nor about our personal sense of truth or morality; our goal here is to understand how the *Beowulf* poet thought about such things and how we can *use* the wisdom the poem records. Remember: the ideas here come not from me, but from *Beowulf*.

And now for the plot of the poem: it's amazingly simple for such a rich, complex piece. By the way: readers on their first time through sometimes stumble with the unfamiliar names. You'll get accustomed to them quickly enough, but if you'd like, to help you remember who's who, just simply them: "Beo" for Beowulf, "Hroth" for Hrothgar, "Hyg" for Hygelac, or whatever versions work well for you.

Beowulf, a young warrior, sails with fourteen friends from his home in Geatland (part of modern Sweden) to Denmark to fight Grendel, a monster who has been plaguing (and in some cases, devouring thirty at a time) the people there. Beowulf seeks and gets the permission from the Danish king, Hrothgar, to undertake the fight, and on his first night there, the monster attacks as all but Beowulf sleep. Grendel kills one man, but the second he attacks is Beowulf, such an opponent as he has never met before. Beowulf, using no weapon, does nothing more than grasp the monster's arm and hold on. Feeling his opponent's strength, Grendel panics, tries to jerk himself away to flee, and in the scuffle his arm is pulled from its socket: because the hero holds on so tightly. Grendel, unarmed, flees into the night.

Both guests and hosts celebrate the young hero's victory. But soon they mourn again: Grendel's Mother stalks them the following night, seeking vengeance. She enters the Danes' hall and kills and carries away one of Hrothgar's best counselors.

Beowulf rises to the new challenge, asking the king's permission to complete his task by killing the she-beast as well. The king, with little choice, readily consents. Beowulf follows the monster to her lair, a cave beneath a dark mountain lake, and there he slays her as well, though with some difficulty. Once again the folk celebrate the seemingly miraculous victory.

Beowulf returns home to tell his own king, Hygelac, about his successful adventures, bringing him treasures and gaining respect and status among his own folk. As years pass, Hygelac's family falls, and Beowulf reluctantly becomes king. He reigns for a peaceful fifty years, until a thief steals a cup from the hoard of a sleeping dragon. Dragons hate thieves, so the beast wakes and attacks the nearest settlement: Beowulf's. Old but undaunted, Beowulf, with a small group of followers, engages the dragon. All his followers but one flee, but Beowulf and his trusty kinsman, Wiglaf, kill the dragon, though in the battle Beowulf receives his death wound.

Having saved his people from the beast, Beowulf leaves them a hefty treasure from the dragon's hoard. But the people realize they are lost without him, not only because they loved him, but because, being small in number, they depended on him— no foreigners would dare attack while the hero lived. They bury the treasure with him as they bemoan the fate that approaches them: deadly invasion by superior armies.

That's it.

Of course, the poem includes more than just a plot. The poet packed it full of other little stories, allusions, and expressions of wisdom that both explain the culture and clarify the story and render the poem more complete by detailing the world in which it takes place. We learn how the people organized them- selves, what they wanted and how they tried to get it, what they worried about, what held importance for them, what made them happy, and what brought them to tears.

Not only the story, but particularly those little added parts that some scholars call "digressions" distill the wisdom that we can draw from the poem and the time. Each of those gems shows not only how people thought in that age of the world, but also ways we may think about our own experiences to get the most from them. You'll also find once again that as people we differ little from what we were then, a thousand years ago, and that in the future—unless we continue to learn and take what we learn seriously—we'll differ little from what we are now. And that little truth, too, will help you do business for as long as we do it as we do now because you'll gain confidence in your understanding of human nature.

And of course *Beowulf* is a poem, but a poem unlike those with which most readers have greater familiarity. It doesn't use rhyme, but it does employ rhythmic patterns and many traditional poetic devices, such as images, symbols, and alliteration (the repetition of sounds) to make its points with emotional power.

And how about the ideas that the poem explores? It's about courage, duty, honor, composure, commitment and responsibility, knowing oneself and one's enemy, understanding customs and history, public speaking, power, and generosity—and much more. Each of those ideas suggests and supports a wealth of applications—as I mentioned in the title, a practical poem, as most literature is when we study it carefully. But then if it were merely beautiful, beauty is more practical than we normally admit.

The Structure of This Book

I've designed this book so that you may easily tackle it in parts, so that each part has an integrity and application of its own, but so that the parts fit together to give you a useful experience of the range of wisdom of the poem as a whole. We'll follow the poem from beginning to end, selecting as we go the most helpful points for close attention. Once we've reached the end, we'll circle back to look at what we learn from the whole thing and pick some general themes and specific points that appear not as part of the plot, but as asides, allusion or maxims in which the poet aimed to capture the wisdom of the time. Each brief chapter focuses on one episode or principle, and each concludes with a "Manager's Spotlight," a summary and direct application of what the chapter covers focused specifically on the needs of managers. Following each chapter title you'll find an epigraph, a line from the appropriate passage in the poem that highlights the idea for the chapter. As we follow the poem in its own order, from beginning to end, we'll select for attention each of its significant points, discussing their meanings and applications.

Most chapters will follow this pattern: "The Idea," "The Passage" (the specific passage in the poem from which the idea comes), "The Application," "Manager's Spotlight." So you'll study what to learn, what the passage in the poem says about that idea, and how to apply it, and then we'll conclude with a quick aphorism that can serve as a "touchstone" to help you recall the lesson. For those of you approaching the text as a group rather than as individuals, following the "Manager's Spotlight" section you'll find discussion questions ("Points to Ponder") to get you started exploring how your organization can best implement the ideas. You won't find solutions for every problem—*Beowulf's* time had no notion of health care—but you'll find plenty of old wisdom that transcends time and place.

When we finish, we'll sum up what we've covered in a list of the main ideas, what they mean and how they apply to contemporary professional life. If you're short on time, feel free to leaf through them at any time and select those that strike you as most pertinent to your needs—you don't have to follow the whole course to find value in the individual chapters. You may, though, need to look back to previous or related appropriate chapters to understand their context. No aphorism stands truly alone. That's why we often find—not only in *Beowulf*, but everywhere—old saws that contradict one another. Contradiction need not create anarchy. We need only understand the point of each assertion and determine its value in given situations, and we'll try to do just that.

Let *Beowulf* help you make the epic journey of your own life a successful one.

1

Mortality and Learning from the Past

By generous deeds one may prosper in any nation.

(i.e., Your own generosity will help you succeed.)

The Idea

Everyone's heard the old saw that those persons unfamiliar with the past are doomed to repeat it.

Like any truism, it's true in part. Most of our thoughts and feelings we share with nearly every human being who has ever lived or who ever will live. Some people reach heights of genius or of love that most of us can only wish we'd find; some experience or commit depths of horror that, if we're lucky, we'll avoid.

Terror management theory, popular now in social science circles particularly because of the rise of international terrorism, suggests that we all seek coping mechanisms that help us avoid falling into a paralysis of fear. It may afflict us partly as a result of the innumerable dangers of the contemporary world, but partly because of our recognition of our own mortality.

Make no mistake: the world has always been eminently dangerous, and mortality has always loomed spectrally before us, more so even in the ancient world than now, when a normal, healthy adult free of military service might hope to live forty years.

The first lesson *Beowulf* teaches is about mortality.

You can't avoid it.

Even if you're a great king who has subdued all enemies, gained amazing wealth and power, and assured a good start to the next generation, you still have a date with the Grim Reaper.

But you can do your best to accomplish a lot, set a good example, and assure that the people who follow you will start their own lives from a place of advantage.

And they can study what you did and learn from it.

The Passage

The poem begins with a brief account of the success of a great, powerful, legendary Danish king, Scyld Scefing (literally, "Shield, son of Sheaf"—names have great importance in the poem, as they often do in life).

"In days of yore" the Danes found Scyld, a mere child, destitute. They took him in. In time he grew up and became the greatest king they ever knew: "That was a good king," the poet says laconically. He "seized the mead-benches from the warrior bands of many nations," terrified enemies, gained fame, and won tribute from all the neighboring kingdoms, assuring peace for his country. In years to come he fathered a son, taught him well, and bequeathed him a great kingdom. Scyld's folk gave him a grand funeral, and his son, who had learned the lessons of generosity, courage, and continuity, in turn fathered a son of his own who extended the noble line through his own children.

Thus the poem doesn't begin with the hero Beowulf or even with his own people, but with earlier generations of Danish kings. The Danes are the people Beowulf in his youth goes to help, to deliver them from their monsters—that's where the "proper" narrative of the poem takes up its course.

Why would the poet begin with earlier, seemingly extraneous events, and what's that business about mead-benches?

To make a point about mortality, continuity, and learning from the past.

Scyld shows us that to succeed in the world you have to be tough and persistent and be willing, as the old saying goes, to pull yourself up by your own bootstraps. You may not be lucky enough to come from a wealthy family, so you have to be willing to work your way up. Where you find enemies, you have to be willing to face and defeat them, though not with cruelty. As the poet teaches later, cruelty breeds hatred, and hatred leads to revenge. You must win allies who will respect you, support you, and not seek to overthrow you.

Then, recognizing your own mortality, you must do your duty. Rather than overindulging yourself and your own whims, you must pass along what you have and what you know to the next generation. You must educate them not only in how to succeed, but also in how to act responsibly. If they don't, your friends will in time turn against them and overthrow them. And they must know that what you've given them isn't simple birthright: they must earn its continuance as you earned its beginnings. They must know when to attack, when to defend, and when to make peace. They must remain vigilant against old and new enemies, seek to maintain and extend the peace, and teach the next generation all they've learned from you and all they've learned on their own.

Even then, they'll die someday, too, but in acting honorably they will have had the best chance for success and will pass along to the following generation their best chance for success.

And now for those mead-benches. In the Northern world of the early Middle Ages soldiers met in a great hall where they sat together on benches to eat, drink, and talk. They drank mostly mead, a honey-wine, strong and sweet. By drinking together they cemented bonds of friendship and martial loyalty and formed tight bands who fought, like the later musketeers, one for all and all for one, defending their lord, lands, and treasures. Scyld probably didn't literally steal anyone's chairs; he stole their loyalties, making them his subjects rather than those of their previous lord. He made them his drinkers rather than someone else's, toasting his accomplishments and committing to his defense. In a sense he was a corporate raider—or a union boss or a don—but with the goal in mind of creating strong allegiances that in the long run would provide safety and prosperity to everyone involved—though to his folk first and foremost.

I'll be explicit on this point: I'm not advocating corporate raiding or racketeering. Nor am I condemning legitimate business acquisitions. I'm explaining what happens in the poem and how you can use it.

I'm also not advocating imperialism, which is hardly defensible, or even preemptive militarism. We don't live now in the same world that produced *Beowulf*, and justifying particular cases in international politics or corporate takeovers would require careful study of individual circumstances far beyond the scope of this book.

But in such passages the poem does teach some general principles that, as well as any in this strange and unpredictable world, can lead to success if one takes them to heart and makes of them prudent practices. Those principles often draw our attention to courage, responsibility, loyalty, and honoring the past, particularly those people who acted honorably.

The Application

Scyld serves in the poem as the model of a good king: strong, brave, daring, responsible, and generous with his folk, he wins their loyalty by doing his duty and inspiring them to do theirs. He begets a dependable heir to take over when he's done to avoid the chaos that, in a dangerous world, can destroy a people—or a company. If we replace the notion of terrorizing one's neighbors with that of earning the respect—and even deference—of one's employees and competitors alike, we have a model for a successful manager or entrepreneur.

If people follow you only because they fear you, at any sign of weakness or possible failure they are likely to abandon you or even unseat you themselves. If they follow you because they trust, respect, and admire you, they just may come through for you in a pinch. You may rise to the top if people think you're better than they are, but you'd better be prepared to prove it at need, and once you get there, you'd better take care of those who supported you. One of the chief tenets of the world of *Beowulf* is *generosity*, particularly to one's followers. If they fear you, but love you for your generosity, you will probably succeed until you lose strength or lose face. If they are committed to you because they believe in your continuing ability to protect and reward them, you are likely to retain their loyalty and support. If they see character flaws likely to beget continuing failure, they will abandon you at first opportunity.

And you must recognize the limits of your own working life: you can't go on forever. You have a responsibility, finally, not only to yourself and your family, but to those people who have depended on you for their livelihood and to their families as well: one accrues that responsibility upon assuming power. That means you must provide for someone to take over for you when you retire or move on. I don't mean simple nepotism, which in the contemporary world often invokes the derision and anger of one's followers. I mean finding and training persons who can not only take over your organization and run it successfully and even creatively, but who will also show the same virtues that got you into that position to begin with. Successful kingdoms, companies, and teams often fail in later generations because control devolved to a relative, favorite, or upstart unwilling to make the sacrifices and exhibit the virtues that won the previous leader his or her loyalties. People are not always born with those traits and under pressure may fail to generate them. The generation in power has an obligation to teach and prepare the next generation to believe in strength of character and generosity to others. Without those traits, a leader remains so only accidentally and briefly.

The same principles apply not only to the leader, but to the rising stars of the next generation. They have an obligation to determine what made the previous generation successful, to aim to exhibit those traits, to resist feelings of entitlement, and commit their own loyalty to those who support them. If you want to inherit power and retain it, you must treat with generosity those who have shown loyalty to the organization, and you must take up the responsibilities of those who preceded you. You must, in turn, recognize your own mortality and begin the process of training those below you who will some-day replace you.

If you think only of yourself and your own career, you betray all those others who have committed energy and lifeblood to the organization's success. You may get lucky and succeed for a time, even for a career, but *Beowulf* suggests that those who do so aren't real men and women, but monsters, and damned ones at that—more on monsters later. For now, let's say that the poet sought to show that long-term success—and therefore peace and prosperity—come not only from exploiting one's abilities and gaining power, but also from wielding it with commitment and generosity, then passing it along at the proper time to those prepared to handle it, those who have in turn learned the virtues necessary to success and who have committed to practice them.

That's where knowing the history comes into play: you should know who had your job before you, what the person was like, what he or she did that worked or failed, what you can adopt and what you should avoid.

The Manager's Spotlight

As a new employee, learn who had your job before you. When you leave, do your best to put things in order for the next person and make him or her feel welcome and prepared.

As a manager, no matter how much you liked the predecessor, make the new person feel welcome. Explain the history of the company and the job and clarify for the new employee the values and expectations of the company. And no matter how much you like the new person, avoid denigrating the predecessor—he or she will worry about being the next one about whom you'll speak poorly.

Set an example of your own on-the-job values. If you expect a lot of yourself and others; if you expect respect from them and offer it in return; if you compete forthrightly in the marketplace; if you remember that nothing of this earth lasts forever, so that you make the most of what you have: you've laid the foundation for success.

Points to Ponder

1. *How much do you know about the history of your company and its values? Make a list of the things you know and of those things you'd like to learn.*

2. *Make a list of the traits that have led to the success of the most successful person you know. Can you acquire those traits? Do you want to?*

3. *Imagine a contemporary* Beowulf *poet writing, "That was a good manager." What traits would the poet be praising?*

2

Weathering the Inevitable Storm

Each must a keen warrior determine to know:
words and deeds.

(i.e., To succeed you must master both words and actions.)

The Idea

Any company will experience its share of storms. Whether from competition, the economy, aging infrastructure, hiring or retention or labor problems, technical difficulties, political vicissitudes, law suits, or intellectual stagnation, every company will face crises. Some not even heroes can withstand: companies, like individuals are mortal. But there's no reason why you have to go down without a fight, and if many people depend on you—or simply if you really like your job and your company—the impetus to survive and prosper is even stronger. And if you make good choices, you can survive with greater strength than you had before.

As Professor Eastwood teaches us through Dirty Harry, we have to know our limitations. That means understanding when you can solve a problem and when you can't, when to hunker down and take a hit, and when to find a "hired gun" to solve your problem.

No organization—and certainly no individual—is big enough and smart enough to face down every disaster. Sometimes you'll need help. When you do, don't wait any longer than you have to: seek it out, get the best help you can find, and pay a fair price for it—but be sure not to give away too much of your organization or yourself in the process. Build a great team. Do what you can yourself. Then hire out what you can't handle and no more—you must retain the loyalty of your own people, refuse to compromise your integrity, and return as quickly as possible to a normal business routine.

Take care: when the help arrives, you must judge it acutely. Don't accept it at too great a cost, and don't deny it to save pennies.

The Passage

The poem moves quickly to the story of Hrothgar, great-grandson of the legendary/mythical Scyld. Hrothgar, too, is a good king. He has won honor in battle, spread his influence, and built a powerful and wealthy civilization. He decides to have built a great hall, the greatest of its time, which he names Heorot ("Hart," as in male deer, a symbol of divine power, or "heart," suggesting the center of the civilized world). He and his folk seem to be doing well, but then their trouble starts.

A monster, Grendel, a foul, hungry chaos demon and denizen of the night, takes offense at Hrothgar's prosperity, joy, and confidence and decides to bring him down. He attacks Heorot, not once, but repeatedly, killing and eating as many as thirty warriors at a time. Impervious to weapons, he appears and departs at will, refusing to allow the Danes to live in peace.

The Danes don't lack courage. Their finest soldiers face a monster that would scare the nose off a hero. They give their very best effort. But they fail, time and again, and the people, terrified, begin to fall into despair, since even the greatest king they know can do nothing to alleviate their suffering.

Sometimes the world gets that bad. Ask any survivor of war or rape or deadly accident. Consult any of the leaders of the world's great religions: life brings suffering. If you don't agree, count yourself one of the luckiest persons in the world and hope your luck continues, and God bless you.

Well, Hrothgar gets lucky: the greatest hero of his time, a young man named Beowulf, son of Ecgtheow, from a tribe called the Geats, subjects of King Hygelac, turns up to solve his problem. He wants to fight the monster—all by himself.

And he asks for no great reward—only fame and glory, the tender of heroes in that age of the world, and to repay Hrothgar for a past generosity to his father: the king had once sheltered Ecgtheow in his time of need.

The Danes had always thought Hrothgar a good and generous king, but in this instance generosity twice pays off for him: for his having helped a fugitive traveler once upon a time, he gets Beowulf's help with his seemingly insoluble problem. For granting Beowulf the right to fight the monster, he may eliminate the problem. All he need offer in exchange is the fame Beowulf desires, so that his name will survive with honor.

That's a pretty good deal for Hrothgar, especially considering none of his soldiers, no small number of heroes among them, can get the job done. He loses nothing in the exchange and gains an even greater reputation as a smart, generous king even if Beowulf loses, though particularly if he wins. And he has a great new ally.

The Application

Hrothgar must take care not to give away too much power and influence to the charismatic young hero, but he must not let a great opportunity to solve his problem slip by. He knows something about Beowulf, his family, and his king, all admirable folk. But he must still make a decision and trust it. He sizes up Beowulf, judges him truthful and of good character, seeking exactly what he says and no more.

There's no substitute for being a good judge of character. If you're not, surround yourself with people who are, or at some point you'll set yourself up for disaster.

And never promise too much. Hrothgar doesn't.

On the other hand, when Beowulf succeeds—he does defeat the monster in combat—Hrothgar rewards him with treasures far beyond anything he promised. He pays well for a job well done. In fact, Hrothgar and Beowulf exchange treasures, cementing not just a personal friendship, but a bond between peoples that each assures the other will last at least the duration of their lives. It does.

Hrothgar chooses well, but in a position from which he can hardly lose. If Beowulf were to fail and die, Hrothgar would owe nothing to Beowulf's king, Hygelac, or his family: the young man asked a boon, got it, performed honorably, but failed—that, in the world of the poem, can happen to anyone and brings no shame or obligation to anyone.

Having chosen well, he acts more generously than the situation requires of him, enhancing his own status and reputation and even perhaps drawing to him additional allies who would like to benefit from his generosity. Having to rely on outside help will in this instance probably not draw enemies hoping to exploit his weakness—they know that none of them could have defeated Grendel—and without that drain on his power, and with an additional committed and able ally, Hrothgar will grow stronger than he was before.

Hrothgar weathers the storm. Luck serves him, but he doesn't let pride or greed get in the way of his using it to advantage. He accepts help when he needs it, trustworthy help, and he rewards that help liberally without shaming his own folk, who through no fault of their own can't accomplish a task nearly beyond human abilities.

The Manager's Spotlight

Hrothgar makes sure that his hired gun is unimpeachably honorable. He outsources the Grendel job, but without giving up what his own people need: he places responsibility to them first. He allows the visitor to risk his life, and the visitor thanks him for it!

Later Hrothgar makes an error. He says that he thinks as highly of Beowulf as though the young man were his own son. Someone could take those words to mean that Hrothgar will bequeath his kingdom to Beowulf should the young man want it. Bad idea. His wife, the queen, intervenes, and subtly asks Beowulf if he will protect their sons, should they ever need help. At that stage, lucky for Hrothgar, Beowulf shows that he was telling the truth all along: he did come to Denmark only for fame and glory, not to determine if he could take over, and he will try to serve the princes at their need. The lesson we learn from Hrothgar: pay well, but not too much; grant honor and reward, but keep your kingdom for the folk who have devoted their life, not just one adventure—however impressive—to it.

Points to Ponder

1. *What criteria help you to determine when outsourcing is necessary and when it actually undermines your long-term credibility?*

2. *How will you determine when—and how far—to trust the "hired gun"?*

3. *What strategies besides outsourcing can help you "weather the storm"?*

3

Be Bold, Be Bold

Quickest is best to make known whence you've come.

(i.e., Tell people what you want and why.)

The Idea

We can say a lot more about the Grendel episode in *Beowulf*. Many readers on first approaching *Beowulf* find the hero arrogant, almost insufferably so. But what we may tend to call arrogance, the folk of Beowulf's time would have considered bold forthrightness, a necessary trait for a hero. Like a pool player, Beowulf must "call his pocket": he must explain the deed he wants to accomplish, tell how he'll do it, and show unflagging confidence in his ability to fulfill his boast. Without those proper, standard steps, he will meet a stern rebuff—no one will believe him, and he'll never get a chance to strut his stuff.

Remember Muhammad Ali, when he first appeared on the athletic scene as Cassius Clay—if you're not old enough to remember, watch some old film clips or ask someone who is. From his first successes he was brash, loudly demonstrative, supremely confident; he demeaned his opponents and proclaimed his own greatness.

Some people loved him; many hated him.

Then with brutal, artful *elan* he achieved nearly everything he predicted.

Now we think of him as "The Greatest," one of those few men, along with Elvis, Arnie, Yul, and Tut, with whom the Twentieth Century most associated the name "King." His words were bold, and he backed them up with deeds.

I remember when I was about ten years old asking my uncle about his job, what he did, what he wanted to do. He told me about his activities, responsibilities, and goals, and without hesitation he said, "I'm good at my job." That surprised me. I had always learned that arrogance is a sin. But he didn't utter that brief sentence pompously, just matter-of-factly, so I had *to think a lot about what he'd said and what I thought I'd learned.

Some people will tell you, "It isn't bragging if you can do it." I'd amend that to say, "It isn't bragging if you say in a dignified way what you believe you've worked to accomplish." If you're talking out of your head and get lucky and win, you were still bragging. But if you've prepared diligently, and you're explaining what you intend to do, and it falls within your capacities, you're simply being truthful—and admirably bold.

People need to know that you believe you can succeed. If you approach a job and say, "Maybe I can do that; I'm not sure," but someone else says, "Yes, I can do that; I've prepared for it, and here's how," who do you think will get the job?

Don't confuse boldness with foolhardiness. But do remember that a convincing boldness can get you what you want. Remember, too, that the first person to convince that your boldness has merit is yourself. Convince yourself through diligent preparation. Then show your confidence to the world, without overstepping boundaries.

In most instances denigrating your competition is overstepping a boundary. Yes, the *New York Times* has reported that negative campaign ads often work. That speaks as poorly of the audience as it does of the politicians generating them. But over the long haul they show only the perpetrators' viciousness and mendacity, which history typically uncovers—often too late to help a gullible public. Even at best, such behavior creates enemies. The world provides us enough enemies without our making a special effort to acquire more. So even when we present our own merits, we do our best to avoid insulting opponents.

Now I'm going to offer two exceptions to that principle. One occurs commonly enough in debate or argument (*argument* as distinguished from *quarrel*—no one wins a quarrel). To win an argument, one must not only present one's own side, but refute the other side. Good debaters can (and should) normally do that without insult, but sometimes the opposing argument is so ridiculously stupid that one can hardly address it without uncovering the blithering idiocy of the speaker. The second occurs in a special instance of which we have a perfect example in *Beowulf*. It is not a common occurrence except in particular cultures of which the medieval north is an example.

Occasionally the literature gives us examples of ritual insult matches. American teens in some geographical regions engage in them for entertainment, usually beginning with something like "Your mother's so ugly that" and continuing with an image or analogy that's supposedly funny, and more often than not is at least witty. Two persons trade such barbs until one can think of no retort, resulting in the other's victory.

The Germanic name for such a contest is *flyting*, an insult match. In the old world people engaged in them as a way of establishing power in relationships. In *Beowulf* such an incident occurs in part to determine if Beowulf is worthy of the task he asks Hrothgar permission to perform.

Where insults serve a social purpose, we seem to accept them as part of the human experience. The ancients apparently revelled in them. But sometimes they caused more trouble than they were worth. Anyone taking them too seriously risked causing his opponent to lose face and perhaps feel obligated to trade blows instead of words.

As with any skill, one had to know when to be bold, when to back off. That's the main question of this chapter, for Beowulf and for us.

The answer is: be bold when what you want to accomplish requires courage and commitment, when you have a natural capacity for the task, knowledge of how to perform it, and intense preparation to complete it, when you are unlikely to have your chance for glory or unlikely to survive without it, when others are in more danger if you fail to *try* than if you fail.

The Passage

When Beowulf and his troop first arrive by ship on the Danish shore, a coast guard meets them and questions them. He is obviously impressed with Beowulf's size and demeanor and compliments him, but demands that they tell him who they are and what they want.

Beowulf immediately and politely identifies his nation and his king, assures the man that they come on a friendly mission, to do his king a service, and even has the prudence to ask the man's advice—what can he tell them about Hrothgar's "problem"?

That's worthy of an aside: asking advice can sometimes create an ally, because you show that you value someone's opinion. On other occasions, auditors may take it as disingenuous or even as a weakness—the situation dictates. The trick seems to be this: if you're asking something you couldn't know, you're safe; if you're asking something you should have known, you've failed; ask an opinion when the auditor can gain honor by answering, but you will lose none by accepting.

Having introduced potential for the coast guard's reply, Beowulf without pausing for an answer boldly asserts that he can teach Hrothgar a way to solve his problem.

The coast guard, like his king, must also be a person of shrewd judgment. He accepts Beowulf's explanation and offer, warning that the speech is often easier than the deed. He leads them to Hrothgar himself, appointing his own retainers to guard their ship.

At Hrothgar's hall, Heorot, the Geats meet another guard, a herald, who also asks their identity and aim. This time Beowulf gives his name and asks that he may identify his mission to the king directly. The king, recognizing the name, admits him—the fact that Beowulf shares the name of Hrothgar's grandfather probably doesn't hurt, when we consider the superstitious nature of the medievals. Then the hero boldly and formally states his mission to the king.

He wants to fight Grendel. Alone. Without weapons. Grendel doesn't know how to use weapons, he reasons, so he should forgo them to give the monster a fighting chance.

Hrothgar subtly reminds Beowulf of his dealings with his father, hinting at an obligation to repay his help, but he also warns of the considerable danger of facing Grendel. He doesn't specifically grant Beowulf's request, but asks the hero to join them at feast.

There one of Hrothgar's heroes, a proud man named Hunferth, asks Beowulf what at first looks to be a simple question: Are you that Beowulf who contended at sea (scholars argue over whether it was a swimming or rowing match) with Breca? You boasted you'd beat him, and you lost?

That simple question serves as a ritual challenge to an insult match, a flyting. You boasted, the man says, and failed— a daring but appropriate volley. As a reader you may get the sense that Beowulf must pass this test before Hrothgar is willing to say, yes, go ahead and tackle the monster for me. Hrothgar needs to know if Beowulf is not only bold enough but smart enough to outwit one of his own heroes.

Now we may expect Beowulf to refute Hunferth's claim and make a similar sort of retort: no, I won that match, but I've heard that you once made a boast you didn't keep. But that isn't exactly what he does. He says, not only did I win that match, but while doing so, struggling mightily with the sea, I cleared those waters of sea monsters, and what's more, you, sir, are a brother-slayer.

In schoolyard language that's going right to the triple-dog dare.

Beowulf boldly, perhaps overboldly, not only refutes Hunferth's claim, suggesting the man must be drunk, but also accuses him of the worst crime the medieval Germanic world knew, one that can't be avenged: one can't rightly conduct blood-feud against one's own blood, and Beowulf's society is governed by the laws of blood-feud.

Ever wonder where the Hatfield-McCoy business came from?

In the argument match Beowulf cuts right to the jugular, leaving Hunferth speechless. He wins the match, but in doing so delivers such an insult—particularly if it is true—that Hunferth has two choices: he must back down or fight.

He backs down.

That tells us something about Beowulf. He knows the truth, knows what he's doing, and has a sufficiently intimidating presence, when he needs it, that even in his youth he can reduce a proven hero to silence.

That's when Hrothgar resolves to grant Beowulf his boon.

Beowulf's boldness pays off.

It pays off again in the fight with Grendel: Beowulf doesn't know it, but weapons wouldn't have helped him anyway, since the monster is impervious to them.

Boldness works when you can back it up, but that takes courage. When he makes his request, Beowulf says, if I fail, you won't have to worry about a funeral: he knows Grendel eats his victims.

The Application

In business as in monster fighting, sometimes you need to be bold. You make money by investing both it and your own invaluable living time. Not everyone will become a hero or a millionaire, but many people can find a better job, enjoy it more, and find in it greater success with a greater degree of boldness.

I'm not counseling uncontrolled investment in the stock market, nor am I suggesting an orgy of job-hopping or plunging into the production of a smorgasbord of new products.

Like Beowulf we do best to foray into new tasks with careful preparation, once confidence of success is reasonable rather than a pipe-dream. But once you've prepared, commit yourself to a bold, honest, energetic run for success.

When you face a competitor, you'll do best if you know strengths and weaknesses, and when you have the chance to win, put the win away: make it certain.

Importantly, Beowulf and Hunferth don't feud. Before a later battle, Hunferth offers Beowulf his heirloom sword, a generous gesture of reconciliation, and Beowulf graciously accepts. Though the sword doesn't help him, he praises it when he returns it, granting public honor to the man he so fully defeated, mitigating the damage he's done.

Today's winner may be tomorrow's loser, and everyone sooner or later needs allies. We never know who they will be. When you can win, be bold and win; if you can help the loser save face, always do it. That doesn't mean you shouldn't enjoy your victory; Beowulf does, and so should you. But we do best to avoid belittling those who failed to win or even compete: the honor we receive comes not only from our own hearts, but also from them.

And what are we to do with Beowulf's refusal to use weapons, his goal to fight fairly against Grendel? Does anyone in business (politics? egad) really play fairly? Aren't we out to make as much money as we can, to find whatever edge we can to compete and win, to grind the competition into dust and out of business? Beowulf does that to Hunferth.

Look at businesses that have broken the law to compete and win—what does fair play mean to them? Sometimes they've won; other times they've been caught and ruined, and the perps have gone to jail. Worse than that, they failed their employees and their communities, taking innocent persons down with them.

Beowulf offers no greater lesson than this one: with power comes responsibility, and responsibility includes fair play. The person who shirks responsibility is far worse than the person who can't summon the courage to lead at all. The poem never insults those who try and fail; it does condemn those who rise to power, use it only to abuse those they should protect, and hoard wealth at everyone else's expense.

Like Hrothgar, Beowulf gets lucky: his choice to fight fairly happens to lead to his victory. More than that: it leads to far greater honor and a crystal-clear conscience. More than that yet: he stays true to his own nature. His strength is in his body, his heart, his mind, not his weapons.

But as we shall see ahead, boldness must have its limits.

The Manager's Spotlight

Boldness comes from strength and well-earned confidence, but with it goes prudence.

A good manager is both traditional and creative. You must know what has worked and failed in the past, proceed prudently in the pres-

ent, and leap boldly where no one has leapt before into the future. Know but beware of trends, but don't be afraid to make even wild guesses about the future. You need not act on those guesses, but from guesses come experiments, from experiments come plans, and from plans come the successes of the future. Of one thing you can be sure: things will be different than what they are now. The bolder and more creative your guesses, the more likely you are to lead successfully when the future becomes the present.

Some managers are afraid to encourage those who work for them to think too boldly and creatively. They fear being perceived as frivolous and they fear someone else's creativity outstripping theirs. Remember: especially as a manager you work not just for yourself and those above, but also those below you, your customers or clients, and, if you do well, for your family, everyone in your community whose livelihood improves when your company profits, and for the generations to come whose lives will depend on your not having made a mess of the world. You must be willing to share the glory if you win, shoulder the blame if you lose. You have more responsibility than you think.

So take a deep breath, get a drink of water, and try to control your blood pressure.

Points to Ponder

1. What was your company's first product or service? What is your top product now? Imagine three possible products that may keep your company alive in the future. Think boldly: make them as innovative as you can, even if they seem impossible.

2. Describe a case in which a manager you know was too bold. Describe another in which someone wasn't bold enough. Which had worse consequences? How?

3. *Consider a confrontation you've experienced or observed. Would it have gone better if those involved had exhibited greater boldness or greater prudence?*

4

Be Bold, Be Bold, Be Not So Bold

Fate oft preserves the undoomed one, if his courage holds.

(i.e., Your fate may save you, if you're lucky and brave.)

The Idea

In this chapter we'll consider the actual fight that Beowulf has with Grendel.

Grendel is enormously strong, as strong as thirty men, with sharp claws and teeth, and the light from his eyes is sufficiently terrifying to set a hero to whimpering.

Beowulf is also strong. The poet will hint later in the poem that Beowulf is also as strong as thirty normal soldiers—that is, just as strong as Grendel, but without the other weapons.

But he has a weapon Grendel doesn't have: he is rational, knows when to be bold and when to be not so bold. And he can keep his composure. They make a good match.

That's the chief message here. Boldness doesn't always work, but composure will nearly always help.

Yes, we can allow that sometimes pure, unbridled emotion wins the day.

But when boldly throwing yourself into the fray isn't an option, aim to keep your wits about you, even in the clenches.

The Passage

After a night of feasting the Danes and their guests fall asleep. Imagine that: you know a human-eating monster lurks outside your door, and you blithely drop off to sleep: that's the warrior ethic for you. Before long Grendel approaches over the misty moor. Then comes Grendel, near to the hall. Then comes Grendel, up to the door, and kapow! with one touch he bursts the door wide open.

He reaches down and grabs the nearest man, tears him to bits, drinks his blood, and consumes him to the last atom.

Then he grabs for another. But on the second try he gets a wakeful Beowulf.

Beowulf grabs him in return, sitting up on one arm.

Grendel feels such a grip as he has never felt before, senses a courage such as he has never sensed before, and does what any sensible monster would do.

He tries to run away. But he can't.

Beowulf holds on.

That's all.

No weapons, no punches, no wrestling holds, no kung fu, no taunting. He could have gone wild with fear, blood-lust, adrenaline, desire for victory—no ordinary foe, Grendel. But Beowulf remains composed and holds on.

Grendel, on the other hand, goes mad with fear. He tries with all his might to yank himself away from Beowulf's grip, but the hero holds on. He keeps his composure, avoids becoming too bold, and his courage holds.

"Fate often preserves the undoomed one, if his courage holds," Beowulf has told us.

And mad Grendel, pulling away, feels his arm ripped right out of the shoulder joint. As he runs, bleeding, howling, into the night, Beowulf remains with the monster's arm in his grasp, a sickening treasure. Following would get him nowhere. He's won simply by holding his ground.

The Application

This chapter, of course, expands on the last one. Beowulf has shown himself bold in readying for battle. Then we see a case in which he succeeds by being not too bold. Realizing that he has the advantage of courage, he acts with amazing prudence. Grendel's teeth or claws could have shredded him had he pressed his advantage. He lets the monster destroy himself. The great source of fear, the *bete noir*, the chaos demon, has succumbed not to superior strength, but to superior courage and composure.

Remember the bully on the schoolyard? Sometimes he really was a tough guy, but sometimes he so intimidated other kids by grimacing, dancing around and waving his fists, rolling his eyes and shouting curses and threats as though he were trying to out-gorilla a gorilla, that other kids rolled over and took a beating or gave up their lunch money without a struggle, fearing not only a beating but an apocalypse.

Those tactics remain a major part of business, politics, and most other professional arenas. Sometimes you're simply overwhelmed, and you get eaten—few heroes could tangle with Grendel and live to brag about it. But Beowulf shows us how to survive. Chess players have a technique to deal with radical attack strategies: they attack even more aggressively. That may work. Beowulf gives us another example. When competition gets too tough, when the market teeters, pressure from outside agencies gets too great: keep your composure and hang on. Rely on your strengths, and do what you do best. Save "bold" for when you're once again on solid ground. Beowulf does that, too, when he faces his next battle, which we'll discuss ahead.

Meanwhile, consider: when is bold **too bold** and therefore dangerous rather than prudent? Mainly, when you have little to no knowledge of your competition and you have reason to doubt your own abilities. Beowulf believes in his own strength, but he doesn't fully know his own strength until he has passed this test. Passing this one, he may treat the next one more boldly. But often, with many human beings making up a company and complex factors influencing a market, we don't even fully know our own strength.

Socrates said, "Know yourself." Thomas Carlisle said, "Know what thou canst work at"—not perfectly grammatical English, but maybe even a better point than Socrates'. If you don't fully know your strength, your first action should be enough self-analysis to determine your strengths, resources, allies, and creative potential. You need to make sure you really know what you want to be and do. Do the analysis honestly, and be bold—but not too bold—in assessing your prospects, but be careful:

your strengths may not turn out to be what you think. We'll see that also in Beowulf's next battle.

Once you've assessed, then you must trust yourself and plunge ahead: taking the chance to fail, you also take the chance to succeed. The latter doesn't come without the former. As Gandalf says in Tolkien's *Lord of the Rings*, it's all a matter of how you choose to spend your time before mortality catches up to you, anyway.

The Manager's Spotlight

Your key here is to let reason outweigh ego. Personality is the struggle between egotism and insecurity—we're all stuck with personalities, but we need not enslave ourselves to them. When conditions say "be bold," be bold; when they say "hold on," hold on. Commit to the option you choose, remaining poised to change as circumstances change. The price of success, as it is of freedom, is eternal vigilance. You can't succeed and remain successful without energetic attentiveness. But if you do it in the spirit of fun and accomplishment, like a good athlete who loves his or her sport, the vigilance can enliven you rather than enervate you.

Let's say you want to go to your boss with a new, creative idea. You can be fairly sure that, if it's a good one, you'll frighten the boss, who won't want to trust your idea and may not even want it to succeed, since you came up with it. You must decide if it's worth trying anyway (if you have a good boss) or if you should save it for a better time (when you have a better boss or you're in charge). Meanwhile, keep your composure.

If you are the boss, and someone comes to you with that earthshaking idea, be generous and give it a whirl, and be glad that your employee thinks highly enough of you to trust you with it. Give due credit and

realize that you're at least partly responsible for that person's train-
ing and for having created the environment in which such a great
idea can emerge.

Points to Ponder

1. *In your working environment who or what is your Grendel?*
   Should you attack (or defend) boldly or cautiously, or should you
   simply watch and wait?

2. *How do the most successful persons/companies in your field*
   compete? What techniques do they use, and which work best?

3. *For Beowulf the "ethics of competition" is enormously impor-*
   tant. Sketch out your own idea of the ethics of competition.
   Discuss them with friends or colleagues—those you trust.

5

The Trophy on the Wall
or
It Ain't Over Till It's Over

That was a clear token, Grendel's claw,
under the vaulted roof.

**(i.e., Trophies are good,
but self-confidence is even better.)**

The Idea

We humans love trophies, medals, mementos, souvenirs, items big or small to embody and remind us of our victories, accomplishments, and adventures.

Some persons find greater value in the trophy and the sense of winning it represents than in the material/financial rewards victories bring.

Others find the greatest value in the process, the engagement in life that takes place as they learn, practice, improve, compete, win, and prepare to compete again.

Beowulf places little value on personal material reward. He seeks fame and glory for himself, but he promotes peace and prosperity for his people and their neighbors. We learn almost nothing specific from the poem about his internal life, his thoughts and feelings. He seems drawn to try to accomplish the most herculean tasks and fight the most terrifying enemies partly because victory brings a kind of immortality—stories will recall his greatness in ages to come—but also out of a sense of who he is. He appears to want neither vast wealth for personal disposal nor political power to control peoples and events. He represents the ideal hero, fixed, even fixated, on heroic deeds because to him such deeds define his nature. Think of the guy who wears a sweatshirt that says, "I am because I bowl."

Most of us aren't like Beowulf. While some may work for the love of the job, most people in the world of business and industry seek material gain for themselves and their families. They believe that wealth isn't necessarily a bad thing, and they judge themselves at least partly on how they provide for their dependents.

Yet many of us enjoy a bit of display as well. Think of colleagues who have golf-league trophies, basketball trophies, volleyball trophies, diplomas, photos, ribbons, mementos of their children's accomplishments conspicuously arranged in their work spaces. Though such items may seem a bit sappy or annoying to those not connected with them, for the displayer they may build confidence, calm worries, or encourage new achievements.

But we must take care to exhibit at least a modicum of taste.

The Romans said, "De gustibus non est disputandem," essentially, there's no disputing matters of taste. That's partly right. Occasionally we must dispute them, and that's a good thing.

Sometimes display is simply grotesque. In Joseph Conrad's

short novel *Heart of Darkness* a character named Kurtz has a circle of pikes surrounding his hut, and atop each pike sits a grinning human skull with the eyes turned *inward*, toward his own view. He's not intimidating visitors; he's feeding his own lurid death fantasies.

Sometimes display gets offensive or encourages bad habits, bad practices, or even revenge. Imagine if your company president had prepared busts of the presidents of all the other companies yours has acquired or driven out of business with the addition of egg on their faces.

Someone would probably laugh at that. But it would still be bad taste.

Celebrating victory and sharing its legitimate spoils is good; we learned that from Scyld Scefing, and we learn it again when Beowulf defeats Grendel. Gloating is bad: it makes one complacent and weak. Creating an insulting display that demeans the loser: that's very bad, because it spurs the kind of hatred that begets vengeance. *Beowulf* teaches us that vengeance begets blood-feud, and blood-feud doesn't end until everyone on one side—and often everyone or nearly everyone on the other side—is dead, violently, uselessly, shamefully dead.

Win. Win bravely, honestly, tenaciously, graciously.

Then celebrate tastefully.

Taste encourages more success and discourages feelings of vengeance. It can even sometimes convince the losers that they lost to the better competitors, which if you're lucky may one day make them your allies.

One more warning: trophies often suggest that the battle has ended; the war isn't necessarily over.

The Passage

After the battle, Grendel flees to his lair to die. Danes and Geats follow his bloody track to make sure he has descended beneath the lake from which he emerged. Then they celebrate: horse races, stories, poems about Beowulf's victory, speeches, feasting, and gift-giving.

And they nail Grendel's arm to the wall above the door to Hrothgar's hall.

Bad idea. Bad taste. One of those times when someone should have said, perhaps we oughtn't do that.

Grendel, the most horrifying of consumers, has finally met his match and his Maker. The Danes believe themselves freed of terror and trouble. They want to debase the enemy who has had them for lunch. Yes, we're talking about rough, tough, unlettered folk who weren't far from a taste for raw meat themselves, but restraint would have shown some useful prudence.

We're not talking here about a set of antlers or a buck's head neatly mounted in someone's den. We are talking about the bloody arm of a just-killed enemy who had in his veins (as well as his belly) at least some human blood—the poet calls Grendel kin of Cain—and who also had a family.

That's right: Grendel has living kin, a mother. And you know how mothers feel about those who threaten or kill their children.

As you might have expected, the next night Grendel's Mother appears for vengeance. Imagine what she thinks and feels when she spots her son's arm.

And according to ancient Germanic law, she has some right: blood-feud, even if you started it, allots a life for a life, unless the parties involved agree on an alternative price.

No negotiating with Grendel's Mother, probably especially after she's seen the arm. She kills Aeschere, one of Hrothgar's best counselors and friends—Beowulf is sleeping elsewhere and therefore unable to defend him—and she departs back to her lair.

The next morning, Hrothgar, weeping, moans and mourns the loss of his friend. Then he explains to Beowulf that, yes, folk had told of how two monsters stalked the misty marches, one in male form, one female, the second just so much less strong than he as is a weaponed woman-warrior than a man. In the Northern tradition, that's still pretty strong, and trained women warriors may wield their weapons with as much skill as do the men.

Simply: they should have known she'd come. They let down their guard, and another Dane loses his life.

Vigilance!

The Application

Even when you think you know your competitors, you have to remain aware of their development and diversification. Even if you think you've driven them from your market, they may have subsidiaries or develop other avenues by which to renew competition. Another company that has long had a reputation for inferior products can, under new management or with better labor or technology, improve its ability to compete and send you scrambling to work if not for cover.

I've met people in business and industry who still don't understand the need for basic research. They figure that as long as current products are doing well, outstripping the competition and continuing to work for satisfied customers, the company need not "waste" money/time on developing new products for a market that may never arise. Basic research makes necessary guesses into the changes that lie ahead and imagines products to meet changing needs—these days, with the world changing so rapidly, hardly any company can do without it, even if financial restrictions impose that it pursue virtual (mind) rather than physical (laboratory) experiments.

Ninety percent of the wisdom of the ancients focused on realizing—in the sense of making clear we know it's *real*—that the only constant is change. The world we knew is passing away, because as we live and learn our understanding of the world changes and we reconceive it in new ways. Science improves, technology improves, intercultural exchange increases, markets grow and fall. What we thought we knew proves to have been oversimplified or simply wrong: think of the growth of physics from Galileo to Newton to Einstein to contemporary work on everything from the structure of sub-atomic constituents to the structure of the universe as a whole.

Some people have so great a need for surety and stasis that they simply refuse to admit new discoveries or consider new ideas: new means terrifying, because one may have to admit having been gullible or even wrong. We save ourselves a lot of trouble if we can avoid clinging to prejudices, stereotypes, and weak assumptions. We have science and literature that the *Beowulf* poet didn't have from which we can draw additional sources of knowledge and wisdom; we should be able to prove ourselves at least so wise as to avert the failings he (or she) found obvious.

When the Danes made a gruesome trophy of Grendel's arm, they invited just-as-gruesome vengeance; when they let down their guard and forgot their defenses, they begged for it.

Grendel attacks them because they had a happy, well-organized settlement; Grendel's Mother attacks for vengeance. His attacks are scattered and wildly brutal; hers is focused and particular.

Don't let yourself make that mistake. The fight done, the war continues; the war done, the world continues, and as long as human beings find reasons to fight rather than cooperate, vigilance remains essential.

Vigilance with generous cooperation (such as the Danes get from Beowulf) may work even better. How long could a monster survive that? Would he even remain a monster?

Monsters, after all, represent something in the natural world or in us: volcanoes, earthquakes, floods, tornadoes, disease; greed, cruelty, overindulgence, callousness, arrogance.

Paraphrasing Pogo, in the long run the greatest enemy is us. When we keep us in order, we keep monsters at bay.

The Manager's Spotlight

Who out in the business world would make you a good ally? Can you make legal, legitimate professional contact without undermining what either company is doing?

What problems does the course of the economy hint may lie ahead? What will you do if they occur? How loyal are labor and management to your goals and mission? How loyal are your customers/clients to you?

Do you look at problems—Grendel's and Grendel's Mothers—as something you need to find, fix, treat, conceptualize, change, eliminate, illuminate, decry, survive? What would happen if through brainstorming you tried to radically reconceptualize a problem that's plaguing you now? Sometimes, sadly, no solution exists to a real problem, but sometimes the problem doesn't really exist at all—or its actual form is different than you've thought.

Points to Ponder

1. *What would happen if you flattened your competition and completely took over your market? Could you handle the result?*

2. *If you already monopolize a market, what events, economic, political, or industrial, could threaten your control?*

3. *What steps do you take now to keep vigilant watch on your market? What new steps can you institute?*

6

Make Peace-Making Peaceful

Then they pledged on both sides a firm compact of peace. . . .

(i.e., War really is hell.)

The Idea

We can make peace with competitors by negotiating, merging, sharing, selling or abandoning a product line, or by grinding them into dust.

Beowulf equivocates on this point, as we'll see in this chapter by comparing two stories, one that appears folded inside the other: what we learn about war from the Grendel episode as a whole versus what one of the "digressions," the tale of Hildeburh, tells us about keeping the peace. Together they address our own nature and that of our competition.

Beowulf is not the sort of soldier to give quarter in battle. He isn't cruel, but knows when he must win—when peace isn't possible without complete victory—and in such a case he aims unceremoniously to dispatch his enemy.

In business that question becomes whether you should crush your competition or collaborate with them. *Beowulf*'s answer seems to be that if you set out to crush, you'd better crush and not fail. If you set out to make peace, you'd better commit to it and not fail. You won't succeed if you attempt either tepidly.

The Passage

Here we'll look at two passages, or more exactly a passage within a passage.

Our larger section of interest for this point encompasses the Grendel fight and Grendel's mother's revenge. The shorter passage, an example of one of the "digressions" in the poem, appears between Beowulf's fight with Grendel and the appearance of Grendel's mother: Hrothgar's court poet sings a song about Hildeburh, a Danish princess of a previous generation, whom her family married off to the prince of another tribe, the Frisians, with whom they were feuding. They hoped to end their blood-feud by linking the two families through marriage, trying to make one blood out of the two them.

But when Hildeburh's family visited her at the hall of her new husband, despite their treaties fighting broke out anew—neither family had fully committed to the peace—and all of Hildeburh's new family as well as some of her old were slaughtered. She could do nothing to prevent the loss of loved ones on both sides. The survivors took her home with the treasures they won from her dead in-laws. "That was a sad lady," says the poet, since she suffered doubly, losing husband and sons as well as brothers.

Both stories teach us that no relationship is simple, and no battle reduces to two participants. Unless you respond in necessary and immediate self-defense, you don't go into battle without knowing the range and strength of your enemy, and you don't assume a battle is done until you know it's done.

On the other hand, when you make peace, especially a necessary peace, you have to make an effort to keep it: it won't come easily, since people slowly if at all forget the harms done to them.

These passages tell us something all too human: we engage battle too willingly and make peace too blithely. Too soon after Grendel's death the Danes assume they have peace; too soon after Hildeburh's wedding the Danes assume they have peace. Peace, the poet suggests, takes as much vigilance as war, and we must do our best to satisfy all parties—even those we've defeated—if we want to avoid renewed hostilities. To what extent, for instance, did World War II grow out of faulty peace-making processes at the end of World War I?

In Hrothgar's case the Danes, unwillingly and without a chance to negotiate, pay a price for Grendel's death. The medievals called it *weregild*, or "man-payment," here Hrothgar's beloved counselor for Grendel's Mother's beloved son. Hildeburh found herself in an even worse spot: she had no choice about her marriage, no choice about both families breaking truce, no choice about returning home afterward, no choice about mourning. The suffering we experience may come from no fault of our own, and the suffering we provoke redounds upon the ones we love.

The Application

Some people enjoy interpreting business as acts of war or as contests in a great arena. Those images are exciting, but dangerous, and we must take care with their implications. What

Beowulf says about war reverberates on other levels as well. Among our actions we need to consider which are serious and which aren't, and if they are serious, we must anticipate what effects they'll have on other people as well as on ourselves. Otherwise, we risk putting not only our competitors but also our own loved ones in the position of Hildeburh: suffering from problems beyond our capacity to mend.

If you intend to crush a competitor, what about that competitor's employees, community, allies: will you make an enemy greater than the one you've subdued? If you wish to crush because that enemy produces bad or dangerous products that undermine a legitimate market, that damage employees, consumers, the environment irrevocably—that is, if you want to play avenging knight—then understand that you must do your best to eliminate that competitor from the market entirely. If you can't, acknowledge that the enemy will spring up again in a new place, under a new name, or through a new market access, so that you'll be ready to renew competition the next time: keep your corporate weapons clean and in good working order.

If you want or need a corporate ally: choose carefully to avoid one with lingering, dangerous animosities or glaring weaknesses, and temper your commitment until you know that ally is dependable in the long term. Avoid potential allies with records of bad business or public relations. If you must ally with someone known for bad practices, make every effort to set the slate clean before you begin operating as a partnership; otherwise, their taint will soon be yours. Many a corporate marriage has brought down a partner who sought it, often the better of the two.

When you make peace with a competitor, either by establishing a cooperative relationship or agreeing to stay out of each other's way, keep to your agreement in good faith. Avoid antagonizing allies for short-term gain, because in the long term you'll pay a big price for breaching either explicit or tacit agreements.

Attempts to look peaceful, then to destroy a competitor from the inside, after the fashion of spy novels, may sometimes work in the short term, but in the long term they demolish any hope of gaining or keeping the trust of other allies. Is one clandestine success worth generations of doubt? Even if you teach other companies to fear you—Scyld did that, right?—what happens once they've grown strong enough to turn that fear into raiding or crushing of their own? Consider where the Danes would be without Beowulf, even though he comes from a much weaker, less influential tribe. Even if your competitors never acquire strength, they are part of the public who will resent your untoward actions and fail you in your time of need—which, since we are mortal, eventually comes to all of us.

In sum: if you must make war, make war and win; when you wish to make peace, make peace, and don't fail.

The Manager's Spotlight

We have a lot to pack into this "Manager's Spotlight." Let's take our discussion inside the organization. Inevitably you'll experience conflicts with aggressive employees or colleagues whose personal professional goals conflict with one another's or with your own. Firing someone is like starting (or finishing) a war. If you must do, either because higher-ups demand it or because you've decided so, avoid acrimony. If you must fire someone for financial reasons, do so with flowing praise, and try to help the victim find leads for new opportunities. If you have troublemakers, make the break clean; don't foist them off on other decent companies, but do give them appropriate but not excessive financial settlements.

Let's consider a rather different example. When you're dealing with internal conflicts that don't require firing, such as relationships between angry colleagues, you as manager have the obligation to sit them down and set things right. If you let such relationships simmer and boil, you bear the responsibility. If someone is the abuser, let that person know you won't tolerate abusive behavior, and stick to your words. If two persons simply have conflicting personalities, let them know that they are in a professional environment and their antagonism may not undermine their work. Do so in as balanced, generous, and humane a way as you can, but insist on it.

You owe it to your organization not to let it fail from within because of silly cases of infighting. Infighting is bad for morale, and it poisons everyone's interactions if it goes on for very long. You, the manager, must to the degree that you can be the peacemaker. You must provide the medicine that alleviates the poison. Cooperation inside improves competitiveness outside.

Points to Ponder

1. *Think about your closest competitor: what would be the ramifications, not just to you and them, but more widely considered, if you put them out of business? What would be the ramifications—not just to you personally—if they put you out of business?*

2. *Think of an organization that to you closest embodies the notion of "monster"; why do you think of them so? If you could legally, ethically, and reasonably put them out of business, how would you do it?*

3. *Consider two persons in your organization who just don't, can't, or won't get along. What strategies can you create to help them, if not to reconcile, at least to work more productively together?*

7

Foreign Waters
or
Really Foreign Turf

Better to make amends than mourn overmuch.

(i.e., After you grieve, fix things.)

The Idea

By now most businesspeople realize that doing business abroad is a different animal from doing it in their own country. They have to deal not only with differences in language, customs, dress, foods, and ways of thinking, but also with changes in time zones, work hours and habits, and assumptions about how business and the world do and should work. We all know the advantage of being on the "home team," but also that we must do our best to succeed when we're on foreign turf.

The keys *Beowulf* teaches to success in a foreign environment are preparation, courage, composure, adaptability, and an ability to resist despair.

We always need those skills, but on unknown terrain they loom larger yet.

Of course Beowulf is already in a foreign country when he reaches Denmark to fight Grendel, but he hasn't really left his native "element": he fights on land without weapons against a foe of approximately equal strength. When he meets Grendel's Mother, he battles amidst a different element and with different rules, and he finds that there he needs luck and attentiveness as much as he needs skill and courage. So he prepares even more carefully than he did before, again mindful that he may fail in his mission.

But he will never fail to do his duty as a hero.

That's perhaps the most important thing we learn from this next passage: know who you are and what you do, and remember that whatever task you find at hand, the abilities and strength of character you've developed remain your allies so long as you stick to your sense of virtue, your understanding of what makes your work right and good and important.

The Passage

While Hrothgar feels heartbroken over his new loss, especially after the rejoicing that had followed Beowulf's victory over Grendel and the Danes' assumption that peace had come at last, Beowulf unhesitatingly takes on the new task. "Better to avenge one's friend than mourn overmuch," he tells the king in one of the many stark aphorisms that punctuate the poem, and he commits himself to a second battle even before he knows fully what he'll be fighting.

We may be tempted to see that promise as imprudent. For most of us it would be, but Beowulf has gone to Denmark to complete a task, and he'll give everything he has to do it. Beowulf understands his own nature as hero, and he knows that only he has a chance against the renewer of the violence.

He has a chance for additional fame and glory, but he also has a sense of obligation: he counsels action as superior to mourning alone.

That obligation leads him to Grendel's mere, a nasty, bloody, serpent-filled lake amidst rocky cliffs. When the party of Geats and Danes reaches its shores, they find Aeschere's head. Beowulf must descend into the water to search out the beast that has taken up the blood-feud.

Unlike for his previous battle, Beowulf dons chain-mail and helmet, and he carries Hunferth's sword, which "had never failed in a fight." Beowulf, without anxiety, the poet tells us, makes a speech, as heroes are wont to do. He asks that, if he should die, Hrothgar will take care of his men, have his treasures delivered to Hygelac, and allot Hunferth his own ancestral sword—essentially, he makes his will. Then he plunges into the water.

Grendel's Mother grasps him, tries unsuccessfully to get her claws through his mail-coat, and hauls him into her cave at the bottom of the lake as the other water-beasts harass him. Though we may recall Beowulf's battle with the sea monsters during his youthful contest with Breca, once he enters the lake he is well outside his element, and then within the cave he must entirely reorient himself. He uses the sword, which will not bite through the monster's hide, and so finds he must wrestle her as he did Grendel. Bent on her vengeance, she doesn't flee—he throws her, then she throws him and leaps upon him, pulling a knife. His mail again protects him. He manages to shake free, look about him, and locate an enormous magical sword, probably the only weapon that would work against a monster largely impervious to them. With one stroke he beheads her. After a quick selection of treasures—most important the head of Grendel, who had returned to the cave before dying—he emerges from the water to his astonished but relieved comrades. The Geats had remained; the Danes, assuming once they had seen blood on the water that Beowulf had been killed, had already departed for home.

You'd think Grendel's Mother would present an easier challenge than Grendel, but not so. Grendel's Mother's courage doesn't fail, and she knows more about her enemy than he knows about her—plus she's got home-water and home-turf advantage. Had Grendel actually *fought* with Beowulf, the outcome wouldn't have been certain.

The Application

Beowulf survives because he prepares prudently rather than arrogantly. Against Grendel, inside the Danes' hall, he uses no armor and no weapons. But fighting in "foreign" conditions he uses both—the armor if not the weapon probably saves his life. When he returns the sword to Hunferth, he not only makes a nice gesture in praising it, but also tells the truth: the sword doesn't fail him because it's faulty, and it is a good sword—a fair complement that helps him assure the Danes that once their flyting has ended, he has no feud with Hunferth. The sword fails because it has no chance of working against the monster: our old, reliable, culturally centered methods don't always work on foreign ground. So Beowulf finds something that does work.

You may say that such an action takes an extraordinary level of awareness of his environment at a moment when failure may cost him his life. That's right. Business negotiations may similarly turn on your ability in the moment to adjust to current conditions, without, of course, giving up your own sense of what's moral, ethical, or reasonable. Beowulf is lucky to find an honorable and effective method to succeed and survive, but he has trained himself to remain calm and aware, to adapt and commit to decisive action. We'll see later that decisive action doesn't always assure success; it may be foolhardy, more arrogant and dangerous than heroic. But composed, practiced decisiveness, particularly in the face of one's demise, may be the only prudent way to proceed—that's the main lesson of this passage.

Once Beowulf chooses to attempt the quest to destroy Grendel, he puts himself in the position to fail—monstrously—and to die. Having killed Grendel, he must answer the response from Grendel's Mother: she has invoked the law of blood-feud, and Beowulf ends the feud by killing her, the last of the Grendel-kin. For his risk he makes great gains: reputation, treasure, and the likelihood that others, knowing the Geats have a Beowulf to defend them, are far less likely to attack his people.

Gaining a high profile in the business world has its perks: title, salary, special benefits, greater freedom of risk and movement. It also brings its share of detriments: when trouble comes, you must be the one to face it, and if you fail, you lose much of the reputation you'd gained. Reputation requires that you act decisively, but humanely and ethically: you have an obligation not to put your colleagues in peril because of your own desire for advancement.

You do, though, have a right to attempt the career you want. If you reach a high-profile position, prepare yourself to follow up the results of your choices with continuing courage and forthrightness.

And when your business takes you abroad, marshal your energies to adjust to local customs rather than assuming they will adjust to yours. You are, after all, the foreigner, and you do better to acquire allies than enemies. They will have the advantage of numbers and local knowledge, even if you arrive as the conquering hero. Get a step ahead of Beowulf: learn more about them than they know about you, and avoid assuming, at least publicly, that your ways are better—even if you believe deep down that they are.

The Manager's Spotlight

As I mentioned at the beginning of the book, Beowulf *doesn't stray from a belief that all actions have overriding moral and ethical components. Yes, we've all heard the old joke about "business ethics" being an oxymoron, but that doesn't mean it's true—some old saws are simply wrong. Yes, generations of businesspeople have got away with flagrant abuses of workers, customers, communities, environment. But the world gets smaller and will no longer tolerate the abuses it once did: more and more actions readily become public knowledge and more powerfully affect larger financial and environmental fields. Even cigarette manufacturers, who long asserted that smoking causes no health problems, now readily admit that it does and (quietly) caution self-control. You must consider the implications of your choices and prepare for the consequences they may create.* Beowulf *teaches us a lot about responsibility, at home or abroad.*

Points to Ponder

1. *Before you make a business trip abroad, how much effort do you make to learn the language and customs indigenous to your destination? Consider: even if you don't* need *to do so, how much would at least a modicum of knowledge help in the long run?*

2. *The general public probably don't as a rule think of typical business activities as "heroic"; how would your job and the way you*

approach it change if you decided to consider your accomplishments potentially heroic?

3. *Think of the last time your completion of a task put you in a position in which you had to tackle an even more difficult task. How did you handle that situation? Did you learn by your choice a helpful technique that you can use in subsequent endeavors, or would you choose to handle it differently if you had to do it again?*

4. *Does Beowulf do better or worse in his battle with Grendel's Mother than in the one against Grendel? What constitutes the greater victory in business: the one against the richer, more powerful foe or the one against the wiser, wilier foe?*

8

Faith and Responsibility

They did not expect to see him again, their friend-lord.

(i.e., Believe in your colleagues as well as yourself.)

The Idea

How much do your co-workers believe in you, and how much do you believe in them? Does it really matter if you have faith in one another or not? To what degree are you responsible to them when they undertake difficult, even dangerous tasks, and how far can you expect them to support you when you take on grave responsibilities?

The main idea for this chapter comes from the passage that describes Beowulf's ascent through the mere, back to the surface after he defeats Grendel's Mother. It defines some of the elements of courage that don't always come to the fore in discussions. It also defines loyalty—another major theme of the poem as a whole. To those people with whom you have naturally or though working together formed bonds, you owe a debt of loyalty, at least as far as they behave honorably. Beyond honor and duty you may choose to maintain the bond, if you wish; to do so suggests particularly praiseworthy heroism. But regardless of what others do, you must continue to focus on and commit to the virtues you believe are right and true.

The Passage

When they see blood rise to the surface of the water, the Danes depart Grendel's Mere for home, assuming that Beowulf has met his death there. Beowulf's men stare at the mere: "They wished but didn't expect that they would see him, their friend-lord."

Beowulf inspects the treasures that Grendel had collected from the soldiers he killed during his depredations, but takes with him only two: the hilt of the sword he found and used to kill Grendel's Mother—the blade has dissolved from the heat of her blood—and Grendel's head, which he strikes clean from the body, which he finds in the cave.

Lingering no longer, Beowulf swims to the surface, where his followers rejoice to see him and give thanks to God. The Lake grows still, Beowulf having destroyed its source of evil, and together the Geats return to Hrothgar's hall. It takes four of them to carry Grendel's heavy head.

In front of Hrothgar and his court, Beowulf tells the story of his battle, and he gives the king his treasures. Even more important, he can assure Hrothgar that he will henceforth have no more trouble from those monsters. Grendel's head gives proof of the monster's demise; on the sword hilt Hrothgar finds carved the story of Noah's Flood, suggesting that people fare ill if they fail to follow God. Hrothgar praises Beowulf mightily, urging him to guard his fame prudently. With a homiletic speech he recalls the story of the bad king Heremod, who through murder and greed finally brought great hardship on himself and his people. Don't be like him, Hrothgar says, but remember the wisdom you've shown and learned, since you, too, are mortal. He assures Beowulf that he will reward the hero well and conducts him to a feast to celebrate the hero's victory and his revenge.

You may find a sermon from someone who has abandoned his benefactor a bit disingenuous. Kings got away with such behavior in the Middle Ages, but I have to agree with you there. At least Beowulf's own folk wait to learn the result of the battle. They can do nothing to help; anything beyond showing moral support lies beyond their power. But I can't help thinking that if not the king himself, some of Hrothgar's men should have waited along with the Geats. All might as well have believed that the blood belonged to the monster, not to the hero, but the Danes despair, probably as a result of their own unsavory history with the Grendel-kin.

Hrothgar bemoans sinful behavior, the sort that brought on the Great Flood, but a Christian audience would see the Danes' despair as equally damnable. Fortunately for them Beowulf either doesn't take their departure amiss or immediately forgives it. He has at least his own folk there to welcome and praise him, the least he deserves for his accomplishments. He even hurries back to limit their worry—how many of us wouldn't take a little time to sort through the treasures before returning?

Of course Hrothgar's sermon offers good advice: avoid avarice and pride. But Beowulf already seems to know that—at least, his actions suggest that he does. He praises Hrothgar's generosity—the king does load him with precious gifts—but urges that they must depart for home to report to their king, which on the following day they do. He assures Hrothgar that should the king ever require help again, he need only call. He adds that if his sons wish to attend a foreign court—a common practice for noble youth—they will find welcome among the Geats.

Beowulf returns Hrothgar's lack of faith with perfect heroism and perfect manners. He could reasonably return sermon for sermon—how could you despair and leave before you knew the true end of the battle?—but he doesn't, showing instead deference to the man he's served and who has granted him the chance to win honor.

Beowulf departs having got exactly what he wanted.

The Application

Don't expect in the business world to get what you deserve; feel lucky if you receive enough reward that you can advance, stay interested in your job, pay your bills, and devote some time to activities you enjoy. But then remember what Hamlet says to Polonius: treat people better than they deserve; if we all got what we deserve, Hamlet says, "who should escape whipping?"

When Beowulf reaches the surface of the mere, his men are overjoyed, and they show as much. The poem doesn't tell us what Beowulf feels—it almost never does—but you can imagine. You've already proven your courage and strength; now you've met the enemy on her own turf and won by your persistence, wits, and ability to remain in the present, attentive and resourceful.

But then as you and your co-workers celebrate your success and survival, you realize that the people who employed you have gone home to comfort and relative safety, assuming you've failed, despite your track record of success, to enjoy the bit of peace you've given them.

They've gone because they assume you're dead.

You're just about to win the Olympic marathon; you enter the stadium well ahead of your nearest competitor. You expect wild cheers of appreciation and approval, and you look up into the stands to find that: everyone but your family has gone home.

Even Beowulf would have a tough time dealing with that letdown. Yet without any show of disappointment he presses on to share with them the glories and treasures of his victory. You persist because your family and friends and king still need you, because the adventure is still worth undertaking, because you experience *joie de vivre* in the attempt as well as the victory. Once again he does "the right thing."

Knowing that he may fail, Beowulf has faith in himself. Having succeeded, he retains that faith in himself because he has lived up to his responsibility and achieved heroically. Athletes who have trained for years for an event sometimes have more trouble dealing with victory than with defeat: having achieved their goals, what do they do now? With the Grendel's Mother episode Beowulf has grown into himself. He must go home and meet his king, account for his actions. But he has fulfilled all responsibilities. He asks no more of Hrothgar than the king is willing to give, offers in return more than he gets: we can hardly say that Hrothgar overpays, when what he gets in return is the promise of the greatest hero in the world to help him again should he need it.

You may well find yourself in a similar position. You may work the majority of your life in a similar position. Make the company a million dollars, and in another week they'll ask, "What have you done for me today?" Beowulf would think that's all right, as long as they're able to offer him a new task worthy of his ability and reward and honor sufficient to his success. You can bet Beowulf doesn't go wanting for anything, and yet he doesn't attach himself too fixedly to tangible rewards. He deals mostly in the tender of the heart and the mind. If you can do that, you'll succeed in business, because you'll always *feel* like a success even if your boss fails to recognize you as you've earned. If you can't make that leap, you'll always—and probably justly—feel marginalized and unappreciated.

The business world isn't about appreciation. It's about struggle and success. *Beowulf* suggests that we live even more in the struggle than in the success.

The Manager's Spotlight

Remind yourself of your successes and your co-workers of theirs. Remind yourself and your co-workers of the company's successes and values. Understand and analyze your failures, but move from them to the challenges ahead, even if you must guess at them: by preparing for eventualities, you will improve your faith in yourself and demonstrate your responsibility to your colleagues.

When colleagues take on difficult tasks, stick with them as long as you can. I'm not saying you have to commit to daily overtime to do a good job. But you must convince them you have faith in them and that you'll be there to recognize and share their successes if you want them to feel responsible to you—and you do, if you want to succeed.

In some ways a corporation is like a body (Latin corpus *means "body"), and you as manager are part of the immune system. Your immune system has a wonderful ability: it will not only produce antibodies to foreign agents to which you expose it, but also guess in producing cells it may need to fight infections it has never met—a remarkable ability that we should extend to our thoughts as well. We must have faith in our responsibility to the system or change the system. Fortunately for Beowulf, he has faith in his system. Beowulf shows us that, regardless of the system, success starts with survival plus satisfaction plus honor.*

Points to Ponder

1. *In which of your co-workers do you have the most faith? Which are most responsible?*

2. *Which co-workers have the most faith in you? Have you demonstrated to them your responsibility?*

3. *What can you do to increase your faith in your company as a whole?*

A question for personal meditation:

Beowulf isn't an explicitly religious poem; it is a symbolically religious poem. It directs our attention to questions of faith and belief and urges readers to consider their actions given their own beliefs. If you are a religious person, how do your beliefs affect how you envision and perform your job? Some people separate them: religion is *there*, and work is *here*. The poet hints that such separation won't last indefinitely: at some point you'll have to square your beliefs with your professional choices and responsibilities.

Good emotional health—and unhindered professional development—requires that you consider the issue, not that you find easy answers, but that you don't fragment yourself with respect to essential aspects of your life. If you're not a religious person, consider how the duties you assign employees and the business practices of your company may affect those employees who are devoted religious people. If you can help them integrate all aspects of themselves, they'll work more happily and be more productive; if you force them to fragment spiritual and professional selves, they'll never work up to potential for you. If the kind of work they do doesn't allow them to integrate the spiritual and the professional, try to think of ways to keep them from feeling as though they're betraying themselves by doing it.

9

Rewards, Emotions, Asides, and Orders

So should a kinsman do,
be open-handed with family and friends.

(i.e., Be generous—with everyone.)

The Idea

Beowulf tells us little about its characters' internal lives, what they think and feel, subjects usually at the center of modern novels and poems. So readers coming to Beowulf for the first time often experience surprise at the emotional exchanges in the transitional part of the poem that appears following the Grendel-kin battles and preceding the dragon-battle climax.

We shouldn't assume that people in that time simply weren't emotional, or that they should, following our contemporary preferences, show a stiff upper lip in public situations and cry only in private. Customs differed. Hrothgar, a strong and influential king, could cry at Beowulf's departure without any-one thinking the worse of him for it.

You've also heard the modern saying, "It's the thought, not the gift, that counts." Beowulf, receiving rewards or gifts for his accomplishments, has no obligation—nor any special desire—

to keep them, but may and should then distribute them as he sees fit. Gifts are for giving, and giving and giving. People saw treasure acquisition as a means to powerful alliances rather than as a way to display wealth. They used treasure for ritual gift-giving, cementing their relationships rather than clinging to keepsakes.

Returning to his own king, who happens to be his uncle—a special relationship, since uncles often took responsibility for rearing their nephews—Beowulf recounts his adventure and gives Hygelac all the treasures he received from Hrothgar, except for those he reserves for Hygd, Hygelac's queen. He shows no undue attachment to material goods, even extraordinary ones—a great virtue to folk of that time, but a strange apparent inappreciativeness to us, for whom presents, mementos, collections, and trophies have great personal value. In *Beowulf* they often have more *cultural* value.

He must also recount the death of Beowulf's friend Hondscioh, whom Grendel slew before he matched strength with Beowulf. The hero tells that story clearly, even gruesomely, and without any particular show of sympathy—a rather surprisingly detached attitude with a whiff of youthful bravado about it.

Readers are equally surprised when they learn that Hygelac didn't want Beowulf to go to Denmark to fight Grendel. If his king didn't want him to go, why would he go? How could he go? People then valued what freedom they had, as we do now, and some could actually use that privilege that we take for granted as a right. Particularly men with status—as well as strength and personal magnetism—could often choose their own course, if they were willing to deal with the consequences of their choices.

The idea here: value free choice as you do your life, and don't readily abdicate it, but take great care with your choices. Select wisely. Your choices affect what you can choose to do and be in the future, and they often affect others beside yourself.

Recently I saw a t-shirt that read, "It's all about me." It's never *all* about you or *just* about you. But we all have to learn when to take advice and when to discard it and strike ahead on our own—that is, when to team up and when to press on alone. That's part not only of growing up, but also of success.

The Passage

As Beowulf prepares to leave, Hrothgar gives him as a reward for his heroism twelve treasures, then kisses him, tears rolling down his cheeks: "to him that man was too dear, so that he couldn't restrain the breast surging"—that is, the king shows an extreme outpouring of emotion. Both men, Beowulf and the king, realize they will never see each other again: Hrothgar is growing old, and Beowulf is unlikely to have to uphold his promise to return at the king's need, since he has completed his task in such an intimidating way that even monsters wouldn't want to trouble the Danes again (their problems will come within Hrothgar's own family instead). The poet does not suggest that Hrothgar's outpouring of emotion in any way represents weakness.

When Beowulf and his troop return to the beach where they first arrived, the hero gives a sword to the man who has guarded their ship, bestowing with that gift a lifetime's worth of honor. You may think that a rather excessive tip, but it shows Beowulf's generosity, particularly toward persons who perform a real service. Even though the man encountered no thieves or vandals, he might have, and Beowulf as a good leader appreciates that point and rewards him for helping without swerving from service to his lord.

When the Geats reach home, they go immediately to King Hygelac. The poet then turns aside for a word about Hygd, Hygelac's queen: she's a good, generous one, unlike the beautiful but infamous Modthrytho, who would order the execution of any man who dared cast his eyes on her. Fortunately her husband, Offa, set her right, forbidding such practices, and Hygd, though young, is too wise for such abuses. Such odd tidbits that stray from the plot teach us about the world in which the story occurs and about people's notions of proper living. In this case: generosity applies to everyone.

Beowulf sits next to Hygelac and answers his questions about the adventure—along with his questions Hygelac reminds the hero that he had repeatedly asked him not to undertake that exceedingly dangerous quest. Beowulf recounts his battles and adds some details about persons at the Danish court. He mentions, for instance, that Hrothgar's daughter has been promised in marriage to another prince to try to end a feud between that family and hers. Beowulf adds a fairly lengthy comment that such marriages often don't work: feuding families will feud anyway. Perhaps Beowulf thought he might win himself a princess in Denmark—he doesn't say so, but the aside itself hints that he must at least have been thinking about the Danish princess.

Then he continues with his own story, recounting the death of his own colleague before he could himself get hold of Grendel. He details for Hygelac both battles and Hrothgar's character and generosity, concluding with the reassurance that he relies entirely on Hygelac for favor. Despite his amazing accomplishments he specifies that he recognizes Hygelac as his lord, a demonstration of humility and loyalty that we may not have expected. Readers, expecting medieval standards to mirror ours, often leap to accuse Beowulf of pride—or greed. But the hero delivers all his treasures to his king, except only a marvelous, magical necklace that Hrothgar's queen, Wealhtheow, gave him, and three horses besides, which he gives directly to Hygd, his queen. "So must a kinsman do," the poet says, show open-handedness rather than malice to family and friends, (and Beowulf gives up every last treasure!), adding that the young Beowulf was in childhood long despised by his folk as a slacker. He grows up to show them something different.

Of course, Hygelac rewards Beowulf's success and the fact that the hero relinquishes all the material treasures. He awards him a famous gold-adorned sword, huge tracts of land, and a home and hall of his own. He doesn't praise Beowulf for choosing to go, but for succeeding, winning fame, returning with honor and treasures, and fulfilling their idea of virtue.

Generosity pays off for all involved: Beowulf gains great reward for victory and virtue; Hygd gains honor and treasures for being a good queen; by being a good king Hygelac gains more treasures to distribute to his followers, and by not overly pressing the point that Beowulf departed against his wishes, he retains the complete loyalty of the world's greatest soldier, a man sufficient in himself to frighten off enemies human or supernatural.

The Application

First, I'll repeat the previous point because it has such importance to the poem and to our time: generosity pays off for all involved. In no time could this theme resound more profoundly than our own, when not just solvency, not just success, but excessive acquisitiveness, often in the face of the poverty of others, reigns for many as a motivation, as if it were a virtue.

In the long run no one will fault you, *Beowulf* shows, if you seek and use wealth honorably. If you acquire it by evil means, hoard it, and use it to abuse others, you become, as we will see ahead, the worst sort of monster. Treasures serve best as gifts to show respect and win friendships and loyalties; they should flow back and forth without hindrance, regret, longing, or misgivings.

You may wonder about Beowulf's gifts to the queen: is he currying special favor or trying to seduce her? He's actually showing the extent of his generosity, giving the proper gifts to the proper person, and rewarding her for being a good queen, as any one of her folk come to good fortune should do.

Second, reasonable display of emotion does no harm and may do much good. *Beowulf* doesn't encourage excess for its own sake, but it does encourage honesty and meaningful human connections. People have a sense for insincerity, but they value the personal touch, the ability to communicate appreciation on a real, human level. If you don't have that skill, develop it, or you don't belong in management. That's not to say you won't be happy and fulfilled in a technical position, only that in organizations people work together, and people working together need mutual positive feedback to thrive.

Showing emotion isn't the same as showing weakness. Yes, Hrothgar is growing older, weakening, and Beowulf is youthful and growing stronger. But Hrothgar is still a powerful, effective king who draws to him the greatest soldier in the world to help him, and Beowulf is still a young man bound in the service of a lesser king. When Hygelac reminds Beowulf that "I asked you not to go," he's showing a hint of weakness—Beowulf can choose to steer his own course—but also a hint of strength—confident in my position, I can allow you freedom and remain convinced that you'll return to my service, because I'm worth serving.

Third, always pay attention to asides, those little pieces of toss-off conversation that are inevitably followed by some comment such as, "Oh, just kidding," or "Nothing, I didn't say anything." In *Beowulf* asides or digressions often clarify the real meaning of the poem; in life they often tell you things you need to know about the persons who utter them, about their true feelings and motives.

Fourth, Beowulf's seeming coldness about the death of the Geatish soldier accompanying him may display a necessarily soldierly detachment and a realistic understanding of the truth of battle, or it may show that he needs to grow up yet. You can't depend on "heroes" to take care of you or to care when you're gone. If they do, be glad and appreciative for it, but in the professional world be ready to take care of yourself as well. Finally, know the difference between a suggestion or a piece of advice and an order. It's often subtle, with the language even reversed. Be sure of which is which before you undertake any extreme action. When Henry II said, "Won't someone rid me of this troublesome priest?" some soldiers loyal to him killed Thomas á Becket. When they returned to him expecting praise, he replied, "I didn't mean that!" and dismissed the lot of them. Did he mean it? The important thing for you is that, if you find yourself in Henry's presence, you must learn a way to find out what he's really asking, and you must remember that any action tainted with dishonor, however much your superior desires it, will return to haunt you. Actions that you take out of honor, explicitly those to help rather than harm someone, may not always bring immediate professional success as they do for Beowulf—he's working for an honorable boss—but they will always allow you to live with yourself, and that's something you can't escape short of madness or death.

The Manager's Spotlight

If you belong to a corrupt organization, your obligation isn't to the organization as it stands, but to reform the organization or find a better one worthy of your loyalty.

If you work for a good boss, you owe that person your best efforts and the proper share of the fruits of your labors—you must determine the proper share.

If you have a good employee, you have an obligation to direct and instruct, but you owe that person the freedom to develop and enjoy his or her work and career—you also owe freedom beyond the workplace. Hygelac doesn't forbid Beowulf to undertake the Grendel adventure; he counsels him not to. When Beowulf returns, successful, Hygelac doesn't offend and embarrass the young hero. He reminds him of both of their duties and praises and rewards his accomplishments and abilities. To do so is not only right, but also prudent. Hygelac as well as Beowulf benefits from the hero's success, and any honor Beowulf wins redounds to his king, and it contributes to greater safety for his kingdom because it discourages enemies. The same applies in the workplace. Selfishness is different than self-motivation. Selfishness destroys team spirit, but self-motivation benefits the whole organization.

Points to Ponder

1. *What cues, verbal, nonverbal, or environmental, do you use to determine the difference between an order and a suggestion?*

2. *Think about the material things to which you have a particular attachment? Are they really necessary to you? Which must you keep, and which could you comfortably discard in a pinch?*

3. *What workplace situations have you observed that allowed for appropriate public displays of emotion? When have you seen emotional displays that caused more harm than good? What makes the difference?*

10

Imprudent Boss, Prudent Employee

Fate goes ever as it must.

(i.e., Stuff happens.)

The Idea

Sometimes you know an idea is bad, but you find yourself professionally obligated to go through with it anyway. Pledging your loyalty to a boss or an organization can help you make enormous personal or professional gains, often more than you can accomplish alone, but it can also place you in position to fail.

Almost everyone has worked on one of those projects that we knew would bomb, but the boss dreamed it up and insisted it would work, so we did it anyway, and we and the company took our lumps. You must make choices about when to follow, when to abandon, and how to deal with the consequences of projects that fail as well as those that succeed. *Beowulf* teaches us that the key to such circumstances lies in understanding and committing ourselves to our notions of virtuous action, sometimes culturally bound, sometimes determinable only in the individual instance. The code of conduct that the poem promotes—courage, loyalty, persistence, achievement, generosity—applies even when the characters are seeking material gain, when they're doing business—though their business is occasionally raiding other tribes.

In later days after Beowulf's return from Denmark, King Hygelac decided to raid among the Frankish tribes on the continent. We don't know if Beowulf liked the idea. The poem does say that he participated, though in a particular and interesting way. Even when he's part of a raid, he doesn't try to take unfair advantage. He does survive. That doesn't to us make the activity itself right. But then we engage in business every day that would make the audience of *Beowulf*'s day cringe.

The main point from this passage—actually several short passages linked together by their facts rather than a complete, clear account—comes from Beowulf's conduct and his ability to persist in tasks long past the endurance of others. The hero shows how, when your boss makes a bad decision that you can't change, you can still behave ethically and survive his or her bad choices. Then, when the time comes, you can make better choices of your own.

The Passage

The next element that we'll treat leaps past the hero's return from the Grendel adventure well into the future. Hygelac, with the Geats gaining strength, decides to harry the Franks— that is, attack them—across the sea.

The poem doesn't say why he does it; Norse warriors did such things. Harrying, or raiding, was part of their lifestyle, criminal to us, laudable to them. That's how they won honor and acquired new treasures for gift-giving: winning them from other peoples in battle. The poem also doesn't specify how Beowulf felt about that idea—apparently that didn't matter to the audience. The passage does, though, exhibit the character-istic way in which he handles himself in difficult situations: with courage, composure, and aplomb.

This story actually begins with Hygelac lying dead on the bat-tlefield, and we can piece the rest together over about the next three hundred lines of poetry. The poet often wove plot and commentary together—rather conversational, if you think about it. Of the Geats only Beowulf survived that battle, and few on the opposite side lived, either. He then swam home across the sea, bearing thirty suits of armor (that's how the poet subtly shows us that Beowulf is as strong as Grendel, but asso-ciating both with the number *thirty*).

The audience wouldn't have expected Beowulf to die with his lord, but to defend him to his death, avenge him afterward, and survive to return to his people, which he does.

We also learn that at the beginning of the battle, Beowulf, walk-ing point, fought hand-to-hand with the champion of the Hugas, one of the Frankish tribes, and killed him much as he killed Grendel: not with a weapon, but with his hand-grip alone. Beowulf has little success with weapons—the only exception occurs when he uses the magic sword against Grendel's Mother. Usually either he is too strong to wield a weapon successfully, or his adversary is impervious to them anyway.

When Beowulf returns, Hygd offers him the kingship—a pret-ty good proposal, considering he has earned it and she herself is part of the deal. Hrothgar says earlier in the poem that should Hygelac ever fall, the Geats could do worse than select Beowulf as his successor. But once again the hero surprises us.

He turns down the offer, not because it doesn't appeal to him, but because his loyalty extends to Hygelac's son, Heardred, who properly succeeds his father with Beowulf's protection. Later Heardred is murdered by exiled rebel Swedes. At first opportunity Beowulf avenges the young king's death, and then, with no other proper heir prepared for the throne, Beowulf, Hygelac's nephew, finally assumes the kingship.

We learn here that Beowulf honors and serves his leader and his leader's successor. He does his job as a hero, wins fame and glory (and considerable wealth) and fulfills his "contract" as a leading member of Hygelac's troop. He doesn't seek a kingship that isn't his, but accepts it when it rightly falls to him. And once he becomes king, he reigns successfully—peacefully—for fifty years. He protects his small kingdom largely by his own reputation and by avoiding creating new problems for his people: he doesn't engage in undue attacks on others abroad.

Beowulf rises through the ranks. Not expected by his people to do particularly well in life, he gradually gains experience, proves himself, works his way up, serves his leaders, shows his abilities, and finally rightly assumes leadership, keeping it for half a century with no trouble the poet mentions—quite a success story, and largely because even when others choose unwisely, he chooses wisely.

Beowulf works, lives ethically, and for a long time survives.

The Application

Human beings live in communities, and we share authority. We don't always have a chance to choose our leaders, and when we do, we often choose poorly. Sometimes we don't get to choose at all. Then we have to decide whether to accept and support that authority, find lawful means to supplant it, or make our own way elsewhere in the world.

The work world tends that way, too. Unless we start our own businesses from scratch—difficult with no experience—we take jobs with companies who have leadership ranks already in place. We join, we serve, we do our duty, we learn, we make progress, we advance, and perhaps in time we lead. Those who rise meteorically often fall that way, too, or cause others to do so. Those who rise by merit, learning as they go and gaining the confidence and respect of their colleagues, have the greatest likelihood of more long-lasting success: they give loyalty and win it in return.

Yes, some bad people gain wealth and power. But they never gain success as *Beowulf* defines it: they always have enemies, real or perceived, waiting for vengeance, and whatever material gains they make for themselves, they steal from others more deserving—bad for the community and bad for the environment because they turn the idea of healthy competition and healthy cooperation into a diseased practice of self-promotion that promotes civil strife. Beowulf succeeds as an individual, but as one who places foremost his responsibility to the tribe: he passes on his gifts and treasures, serves his people, and fulfills his responsibilities, accepting what he earns, no more, doing his best to assure that others receive their proper promotions and rewards.

In many ways Beowulf is the ideal manager. He earns his reputation, leads by example, supports his superiors, assumes authority when it rightly devolves to him, and leads powerfully, peacefully, and effectively until mortality (no retirement in his case) catches up to him.

We can't, of course, expect real persons to be Beowulfs—he's a fictional creation (though many of the characters in the poem are historical figures, Hrothgar and Hygelac, for example). But we can use him, even a thousand years after his creation, as an example, not a model, of the laudable professional. We don't have to be heroic. But if we learn, earn our way, work cooperatively, hone our talents, behave ethically, build loyalties, and extend the effort to win in the marketplace, we can find a good deal of success—if a bit of luck stays with us.

No getting around that. Think of the millions of human beings who have died before their time, who have been crushed under ruthless regimes, or who have never experienced health good enough for them to go out and compete; then thank God if you have the wherewithal to make your mark. Beowulf does.

Sometimes your managers will make bad decisions; your task then is to clean up, limit the damage, and when your turn comes, set things right. Bad decisions you can and must forgive; you will make some, too. Unethical decisions create the big problems: what do you decide to do then? You must decide your limits; if a boss tries to push you beyond them, beyond what you're willing to do, you must have the courage to extricate yourself from the job or the company. You must live with yourself first, and you will have a harder time later in your life leading good people if you're not able to think of yourself as a good person and a trustworthy leader. Your opinion of yourself has as much influence on your success as does others' opinions of you.

So choose prudently and let others do so as well. Avoid putting colleagues into situations you yourself would flee—unless you know they're heroes, in which case you must reward them as such, even if you feel diminished in the process. The company, the community, the world depend on you and me, but altogether they amount to far more than you and me.

The Manager's Spotlight

Think about employees who have "heroic" abilities, not in the Beowulfian sense, but abilities that exceed those of others. Are you doing your best to help them explore and exploit those abilities?

When you lead, do you consult those whose abilities could help you succeed? If not, do you avoid it because you fear seeming weak, because you don't want to share credit, or because no one else in your organization has the ability to help you? If the latter, go out and get some better help as soon as you can afford it!

Remember that if you can help instill a sense of connection and responsibility among your co-workers, you have vastly improved your own and the company's likelihood of success.

Points to Ponder

1. *How have you confronted bad decisions your bosses have made? Could you have done better? Could you have helped? Did the situations call for silent acceptance, counsel, or alternative actions?*

2. *How often do you consider the long-term consequences of your professional choices? Do you regularly think past a "five-year plan"?*

3. *When you make professional choices, how do you deal with their ethical implications? How have instances played out in cases where professionals made choices without ethical considerations?*

11

On Stealing and Hoarding

He avenged that deceit by trickery, the thief's craft.

(i.e., Deceit will catch up to you.)

The Idea

Do you know anyone who cheats on taxes, or who, asked on the honor system to take one free item, will take more than he or she should, or who will without permission bring home tools from the workplace for personal use? Do you have friends or family who have the hoarding mentality, collecting everything and squirreling it away in case they'll need it later?

Most people don't steal in the traditional sense, and most of us don't have enough wealth to hoard in any significant way. But many of us, seeing the contemporary world as unfair, wasteful, and dog-eat-dog, will get awfully close to it. The Beowulf poet took a particular interest in such activities because for the ancient Germanic folk they unraveled the fabric of social life.

In this chapter we'll consider the old world's understanding of stealing and hoarding to show where they caused trouble for the medievals and reconsider how they affect us as well. We punish some forms of stealing even more heavily than we do many violent crimes, yet we've come to wink at others as part of everyday life, even as smart, if one can get away with them. With the rise in public obsession with rich and famous people that we see in entertainment journalism, today we look at accumulating wealth and possessions almost as a spectator sport, worthy of cheers and gawking.

The *Beowulf* poet raises these questions about how we approach material goods: why should we acquire them? how should we use them? what happens if we cling to them? I relate the questions here not to call undue attention to your peccadilloes, but to address a philosophy of life and work that has caused human beings trouble since we first began to evolve the idea of private property. With respect to belongings: we fight over them, spend our better energies acquiring them, bemoan the troubles they cause, and envy their possessors.

This chapter deals with the problems that set up the culminating episode in *Beowulf*, the hero's fight with the dragon. They begin with hoarding, which leads to theft, and finally results in murder.

We commonly hear the word *Viking* applied generally to medieval Norse folk—not a very nice work, actually, since it originally meant *pirate*. Well, many tribes did at least occasionally if not often engage in piracy. They saw it as a heroic way to acquire new goods and treasures: go somewhere and fight for them! The *Beowulf* poet does praise heroic adventures, but the characters in the poem who actually engage in harrying or raiding don't ultimately make out too well: eventually a Grendel or a vengeful enemy shows up to even the score. Further, anyone who acquires goods and treasures for reasons other than sustenance or gift-giving comes to a bad end. The "good" characters give gifts whenever they can. When they receive gifts, they value and treasure them, then in time pass them along to someone else to extend the honor they received from them. The poem depicts those people who hoard as evil, even monstrous.

Yet for us, the goal of business is making money—lots of money—so that we can buy what we want, gain power over the course of our lives, and influence others to do what we want them to do. Must the corporate world reject *Beowulf* as antithetical to its reason for being?

First, corporations don't exist merely to make large sums of money. They also exist to provide products and services that people need or want, and if they don't do that very well, they won't last indefinitely. Run well, they also employ people and serve their communities, sometimes even their countries and the world. *Corporation* need not imply *exploitation*.

Second, *Beowulf* doesn't necessarily denounce wealth or power. The poem praises those who use them well: to support and defend the people and rule generously and justly. It does, though, expose the evils of hoarding wealth for its own sake or using power to oppress others. The suffering that such behaviors cause returns, if not to the sources, to their descendants or others innocent of the abuses. As the Bible says, the sins of the parents are often visited upon the children; the *Beowulf* poet, whether from knowledge of the Bible or not, agrees and gives examples.

We too would benefit from understanding the difference between wealth properly acquired and enjoyed versus excess amassed and abused. That's the exercise of this chapter.

The Passage

After Beowulf has ruled successfully for fifty years, a disaster occurs that sends his kingdom into a panic.

A poor servant or slave, apparently exiled by his master, wandering in the darkness, accidentally finds his way into a dragon's barrow. The Anglo-Saxons tell us that dragons settled upon old heaps of treasures they found buried in barrows and slept atop them, guarding them from human beings so that they were no longer available for enjoyment and use.

The thief, frightened and silent, tries not to wake the dragon: why would he want to, since the dragon would burn him to a crisp with its fiery breath? However, wanting to find a way to reconcile with his master, he steals from the hoard a beautiful cup, with which he returns to make peace.

In those days even servitude was preferable to exile, which in most cases meant a death sentence, since few persons or peoples would take in an unidentified wanderer—likely trouble and another mouth to feed.

In those days, as occasionally they are now, buried treasures were real. In a passage of the manuscript damaged beyond our ability to reconstruct it entirely, we can decipher how the poet explains that sometimes the last survivor of his race, immensely rich with treasures but lonely beyond his ability to endure, mourning his comrades lost in war, will bury all their heirloom treasures together in barrow so that no one can find them, then weep and pine over them "until death's flood touches his heart." Then the wicked dragon will creep into the hoard.

Some scholars think the dragon comes when the man dies. Others think that as death approaches, the man, addicted to the treasures, transforms into the dragon, burying himself in the barrow until Doomsday, unless some unfortunate soul wakes him.

From wherever they come, dragons, so the sources say, had a remarkable sense for the treasures they had claimed as their own; they could sense anything missing down to the last cup, and they refused to tolerate the least diminishing of their hoards, even if all they had done with them for hundreds of years was to sleep on them.

So the dragon wakes, angry.

It flies to a nearby settlement, which happens to fall within Beowulf's kingdom, and burns the village to the ground. It doesn't trouble to locate the thief; its vengeance extends to anyone and anything in its vicinity. And once its ire has been roused, it's difficult to quench.

Beowulf returns to the village to find the devastation. Only Beowulf, even in his old age, has the ability to fight the dragon, and he must do so, though he knows he will die trying.

This passage explains the evils of theft and hoarding. Your first impulse is to say, let the poor fellow have the cup—it barely detracts from the enormous wealth of the barrow. True enough. But dragons don't permit their wealth to be in the least diminished. They want it all, forever.

Further, from the Anglo-Saxon point of view, the thief steals the cup in a cowardly way, surreptitiously, hardly an admirable act. He'd have done better to bop the dragon on the nose and then take the cup. Of course, then he'd have got roasted on the spot. But the poet shows again that while martial heroism is admirable, stealing eventually—if not immediately—brings about bad consequences, if not to the thief, then to many others. Perhaps his lord should have forgiven the poor man—or perhaps he exiled him because the servant didn't understand the gravity of such actions as theft.

The creature fond of hoarding, the dragon, represents continual theft. The treasures, hidden away, haven't the capability of serving their proper function, of joining persons and peoples through the act of gift-giving. Withdrawn from the process of social exchange, they serve no one, and many otherwise good relationships may fail because the giver lacks the gifts to bestow to maintain them—essential to peace in the ancient Germanic world. So theft and hoarding both lead to social instability and war, war that the leader without sufficient treasures will certainly lose, unable to reward his followers and pay for peace against enemies.

From the medieval point of view stealing and hoarding produce, in the end, the same horrible results, not because the perpetrators value material goods, but because they misunderstand their value and so misuse them.

The Application

No one can really answer numerically the questions "how much profit is too much profit?" and "how much wealth too much wealth?" But *Beowulf* answers them in terms of human experience and interaction, in terms of quality of life. A person is too wealthy or a company too profitable when any of that wealth comes from theft or when its accumulation destabilizes a community and threatens its health or survival.

According to *Beowulf* in principle any theft is bad because it misdistributes "treasure": goods should always go to the person who has earned them or who needs them to work or to survive. Theft is the opposite of gift-giving in a society in which peace and prosperity are based on gift-giving.

Hoarding is bad because it denies the *real* value of the goods: sharing them builds relationships that in the long run accomplish more good and build more power because they build trust and cement alliances that far outstrip any individual's ability to rule. Secure, satisfied peoples may or may not serve their rulers, but cheated, abused peoples never will, if they can avoid it.

Here's what that means to you on the job.

We've seen recently a growth of public interest in corporate crime. After decades of near silence on the topic, media have begun again to draw attention to corporate scandals involving billion-dollar conspiracies, faulty earnings reports, insider trading, price fixing and gouging, political influence peddling and illegal campaign financing, misrepresentation of products' health hazards—the list grows practically daily. The lobbying power and anonymity of the corporate structure has tended to dissipate blame rather than focus it on individuals who tend to hide behind the rationale that business is about making money, not about teaching ethical behavior. Those who get caught claim they weren't doing anything wrong, just doing business like everyone else. *Beowulf* shows the fallaciousness of such reasoning.

Any heroic act is a public act, because it helps not only the doer but the public. Any abuse is a public act, because while it may briefly help the abuser gain wealth or power, in the long run it hurts the public, either by evoking direct acts of vengeance or by lulling the public to sleep with respect to its interests and its values. Everybody's cheating; why shouldn't I cheat, too?

An acquaintance recently told me there's no such thing as cheating anymore; there's only what you can get away with. That's the sleep that *Beowulf* resists. What you get away with, someone else will get away with *against* you. As we permit more abuses, we dare more abuses; more abuses lead to greater abuses, and greater abuses produce more and angrier enemies. That doesn't make the enemies *right*; it only makes them enemies. And we need fewer enemies in an age when the world is shrinking and alliances become not desirable, but essential to a business's (and perhaps a world's) survival.

The danger of that argument is, of course, the fallacy of the "slippery slope": if we permit one thing, that leads to a worse thing which leads to another worse thing. I'm not falling down the slippery slope. *Beowulf* does show, though, that small deeds can have large consequences, and that even excellent and successful leadership can't always avert the bad consequences that come from such acts. Multiply, then, the number of bad acts, and we multiply the chance that we'll overlook the one that will bring us crashing down. Thieves and hoarders, even in the guise of proper citizens, keep information and resources from the larger community that may need them to protect itself and survive. While you have a responsibility to yourself to live a fulfilling life, and to your family to make sure that they have the best opportunities to fulfill themselves as well, you have a responsibility to all members of your corporation and community not to eliminate their roads to fulfillment either.

And if a member of your corporation or community makes a mess, you have an obligation to try to help clean it up. Beowulf doesn't even punish the thief who stole the cup from the dragon. He does require that man to lead him to the dragon's barrow, where he himself accepts the task of destroying the monster.

Leadership brings with it special responsibilities, not just for one's own actions, but also for all those in one's charge or care. If an error occurs through no fault of your own, you still must help clean it up, not cover it up. Interestingly, rather than placing blame, Beowulf instead aims to perform his own duty and reward those who attempt to do the same. He even rewards those who fail in the attempt.

That makes the treasure more a gift than a reward. Gifts, as we learn, may bring loyalty or they may not—that's medieval Germanic pessimism for you, or probably just human nature. But without the gifts the community will certainly fail. That's why corporations often bestow bonuses, though more often than not among a select few rather than among a deserving many.

Building wealth and winning tributes—by nearly any means— becomes an addiction. Distributing wealth generously rather than hoarding it preserves a community, if only for a time.

The Manager's Spotlight

Employees may sometimes appropriate company supplies for home or personal use, a practice that in small increments causes limited damage, but in the long run can produce disrespect for the workplace and self-serving rather than community-serving attitudes. Managers, though, must set a good example by not allotting themselves greater and greater benefits unavailable to other employees—that, too, is a kind of stealing and hoarding that produces bad morale and encourages periodic, incremental theft on the part of others. We do lead by example.

That doesn't mean that leaders must always be right—that's impossible for mere human beings. But you must set the tone and set the example, show that you not only believe in but practice the values you want your company to exemplify. By practicing those values you may limit material gain in the immediate present, but you'll extend the life of the company and deepen its presence in the community, bringing more wealth—to share—in the long run.

Points to Ponder

1. *You know someone who periodically lifts company supplies for personal use; what do you do about it? The answer isn't quite as simple as it may seem.*

2. *If you have occasionally lifted company supplies for personal use, what do you do about it?*

3. *Imagine you were able to accumulate all the wealth you want, or at least all a person may hope to acquire? What will you do with it—and what will happen to it in the long run?*

4. *How significant an amount must one inappropriately appropriate for us to call it theft? How exclusively must one protect wealth before we call it hoarding?*

12

On Monsters and Terrorism

Swollen with rage,
he wished to requite the enemy with fire.

(i.e., Understand your enemy.)

The Idea

The specter of terrorism now haunts the world as a super-power nuclear conflict did during the cold war. What effect does the concern with terrorism have on your organization? What effects should it have?

We don't need to make too great a leap to see the monsters in *Beowulf* as terrorists. That's just a metaphor, but it's a pretty helpful one.

When the Danes and the Geats built their societies, they didn't expect attacks from monsters. Those attacks come from no particular fault that they are able to perceive in themselves. And yet they come, so the peoples and their leaders must deal with them.

Obviously, we have no simple answers for *how* to do so. The poem practically suggests that we must figure that out as we go along. It does, though, give us hints about how to approach terrorism attitudinally and how to treat it once it occurs. Terrorism has grown into far more than a political problem.

First, since it is a problem for our world, our countries, our communities, it is a problem for our corporations. Problems have a way of filtering throughout a society, so any organization that wants to remain healthy must consider societal conditions, how they will affect business and employees and what changes they will create in markets and working conditions.

Further, such considerations apply not only to politico-military terrorism, but also to corporate terrorism: vicious attempts by one company to undermine or ruin another or by employees to ruin the company from within.

Ultimately, the poem says that we may sometimes fail to defeat terrorism or, if we do defeat it, its ill effects may still linger. But we have hope if we do our best to meet and understand the enemies, determine to what degree we are at fault and respond accordingly, know the difference between a negotiation and a battle—and make sure we absolutely win any battle, and embody the difference between cruelty and firm, committed response.

The ancient Germanic heroes loved boasting, but they avoided boasts they didn't believe they could fulfill. Having accepted and promoted a code of conduct, they could deviate from it only with great shame and usually with the consequence of vengeance. When the situation turned to battle, they realized that only steadfast courage and great skill could get them through it. They relied on allies who could and would help them and, at their best, avoided making enemies who could stand in the way of victory. When they made laws, they understood the consequences of outlawry both to those who made the judgments and to those who broke the law—or they suffered from the results.

In *Beowulf* the terrorists are for the most part defeated, though after considerable trouble or at great cost. The poet provides no simple answer where none is available. The poem suggests that sometimes terrorism arises from our own abuses, but sometimes it comes simply by the presence of evil in the world. Either way, we must remain prepared to prevent it where we can and respond quickly and decisively to it when it comes.

The Passage

The monster stories in *Beowulf* parallel terrorist acts in our own time. The monsters are small in number compared to the peoples they attack, but they have increasingly greater commitment to the destruction they wish to cause and increasingly powerful means by which to carry out their intentions. They attack, unexpectedly, settlements where the people have become complacent or have lagged in considering where their weaknesses may lie. They hit a settlement, exit, and leave behind the threat that they may hit again, perhaps with more devastating results the next time.

Grendel comes to Hrothgar's hall, Heorot, because he hears the people enjoying themselves with song and laughter. He hates the sounds of pleasure, and he resents the presence of people in what he wishes to consider his own territory. He enjoys terrorizing, attacking, killing, and feeding on them.

We may have a touch of sympathy for the monster's feelings if not for his methods. Quite possibly the Danes' building intruded on his sovereignty without their having even asked permission, but until his attack, they probably weren't even certain of his existence. Regardless, he takes offense merely at their presence and uses the offense as an excuse—and opportunity—to indulge his bloodlust, at which point most readers retain little sympathy for him.

Grendel has special weapons: tremendous strength and speed, great size, stealth, sharp teeth and claws, his invulnerability to human-made weapons, a fell light that beams from his eyes, and the sheer horrific nature of his attacks. Yet for all that he attacks alone against the great number of the Danes. He attacks and retreats with impunity, beyond the Danes' ability to find him and bring him to justice.

Without the wherewithal to fight him, they accept the help of an international ally, Beowulf, who has the strength and means to contend with their attacker. Beowulf wins not by superior firepower, but by superior courage, method, and composure. He knows little about his enemy until he sees him in person and grasps him, testing strength for strength. He fights prudently, without cruelty, but with complete concentration and commitment, and he wins—though the result need not have come out that way, since Beowulf fights without weapons beyond his own body and mind, nothing to match Grendel's teeth and claws. In their fight they undergo, in a sense, a kind of negotiation, Grendel grabbing, Beowulf grabbing, Grendel evaluating, Beowulf waiting, Grendel pulling, Beowulf holding on, Grendel escaping, mortally wounded.

In a sense, the terrorist here kills himself, leaving dead Danes, one dead Geat, and fear as his legacy. Life will go on for the Danes, so Grendel has failed, other than that as long as he lived, he inflicted the terror he sought.

The Danes then assume that, the battle over, the war has ended also. But Grendel's Mother attacks for vengeance, something that anyone who knew there were two monsters would have suspected, vengeance being a part of the social system.

Grendel's Mother has less power than her son, but she has a greater mind and more discriminating tastes. When she attacks, she kills Hrothgar's best friend and counselor, since they have killed the only being she loved.

Again we may feel tempted to have sympathy for the monster. She is, essentially, following the law: a death for a death. But Grendel had killed dozens, maybe hundreds of Danes, so the score is hardly even, and she doesn't seek the *weregild* ("man-payment," a designated sum that will square the social debt created by the crime), the legal alternative to murder for murder. She doesn't want it, nor would most parents, but she has sought her vengeance not through legal means, but by a terrifying act in the dead of night, an act after the fashion of her son's, and the Danes don't know for certain that Grendel is dead.

Beowulf then, too, follows the law: where the other party will not consider weregild, he must seek a life for a life, Grendel's Mother's for Aeschere's, and he must make certain that Grendel has died, so that no more attacks will trouble the Danes.

With greater cunning and greater commitment to victory, the she-monster proves a greater challenge than her son, but Beowulf wins by wit, skill, and luck—weapons that offset the claws, teeth, and familiarity with the surroundings that lend her the advantage. Uncertain of what will happen next, Beowulf must follow the attack to the source and wipe it out, make certain that he has cleaned out the entire "cell" so that no more terrorist attacks will trouble the Danes. He proves the completion of his task with Grendel's severed head, a gruesome, if not cruel, and irrefutable token of his success and their safety.

Later the dragon attacks the Geats because of the theft of a cup—a precious one, no doubt, but hardly a dent in the vast edifice of its treasure. Because of that perceived slight, he attacks indiscriminately, flying by night to burn the homes of people who until that moment had no notion whatever of his existence. He carries the terror of practically super power, and of course the people fear that he has only begun his assault. Beowulf, even given his advanced age the only person with the credentials and abilities to fight such a monster, must take up this new battle, end this new threat of terrorism, a threat greater because more far-reaching than that of the Grendel-kin. When upon his return the locals place the cup in his lap and tell him the story, he accepts the responsibility to defend his people.

Though he would rather fight hand to hand, he must arm with sword and a special fire-resistant iron shield—he knows that otherwise he has no chance against such an adversary. With eleven hand-picked soldiers, and the thief to guide them, he strikes out against the monster, knowing he has little hope of surviving but that with a dragon on the loose, his people will not survive without his attempt. Terror, once unleashed, doesn't go away by itself. Someone must face it and, baring the opportunity to reason and make peace, destroy it.

We may suspect that Beowulf finds joy in such battles. We may be sure that he never shirks his responsibility to fight them.

Some readers say, bad decision: as king, he should like Hrothgar have found others to fight the battle so that he might remain as stabilizing force for his country. The poet does tell us they'll be lost without him. But they miss the poet's point not about the institution of kingship, but about Beowulf's nature as a human being and a hero: no one but he could win the fight; whatever happens to his folk after he dies, they will not have a chance to survive unless he defeats the dragon.

First things first.

The poet alludes to one other event for which we must account in this chapter. We may call it court intrigue or civil war or family strife, but we may also consider it an act of terrorism. In the next generation after Hrothgar's death, the king's nephew kills Hrothgar's son and heir to take over the kingdom, and in the conflict Heorot, symbol of peace and order, is burnt to the ground. The poet wants to make sure that we recognize that terror may come from within as well as without, and internal terror may wreak just as great and long-lasting horror and destruction. It may take place within families, or it may come from previously trusted allies. We must avoid making enemies, but having made them, we must prepare for trouble, then identify its true sources and disable them.

The Application

As it was in the ancient and medieval world, terrorism is now again a part of our lives—for some peoples it always has been. As we know, it arises from a vast complex of causes and may manifest itself in any number of ways, so we can't count on politics alone to solve it—they will more likely exacerbate it. That means that prudent corporations must prepare for terrorist acts and their eventualities.

Corporations can't themselves fight terrorists, but corporate leaders can take into account the likely effects of terrorism on business practices. Can you do anything to prevent attacks on your facilities and to protect your people and assets should an attack affect your facilities? Can you buffer your financial position so that any attack is unlikely to ruin your company entirely? Do you have trained safety people on staff and have you laid out safety practices to protect employees placed in danger by an attack? Can you improve security without making your workplace oppressive to employees?   Do your employees know what to do in case of an emergency?

You can't prepare yourself for every potential problem, but you can at least *think* about likely ones and train appropriate staff to deal with them.

If yours is an international company, are you doing anything to improve communication, assure fairness, and limit any contribution you may be making to disquiet, and are you taking steps to ally your company with government agencies, other businesses, and local communities to make you a less likely target? That doesn't mean you should deny your values or pander to terrorists; it does mean you should try to be part of the solution rather than part of the problem. Companies who abuse workers, customers, or local communities or customs may more likely be targeted, while companies with strong allegiances and strong security plans may, being harder and less appealing targets, remain relatively trouble free.

In the corporate world you can't expect to find a Beowulf to rescue you in times of trouble, so you must take the initiative to protect yourself as well as you're able. Your greatest danger may be merely ignoring the state of the world, hoping the problems will go away, depending on politicians to solve them. While we may hope for rescue, we do best to remain vigilant and creative in our preparations to avoid interference with regular activities, even if for you that means little more than hiring carefully and buying the latest and best anti-virus software.

You can be sure that, if you're extremely successful financially, at the very least you'll have competitors looking for ways to undermine or copy your success, ruin you in the marketplace, or find a way to absorb you. You'll have hackers trying to creep into your computer systems. You'll have a disgruntled employee who tries to take your clients to his new employer or damage your production before he leaves. We think of terrorism as large-scale activity, but small-scale activities can also create irreparable harm. Your best bet is to stay clean, stay ready, and stay ahead of the competition.

The Manager's Spotlight

Think about the "monsters" most likely to stand in the way of your company's prosperity. If you're thinking about the EPA or other government regulation, you're probably looking in the wrong place. If you seek to avoid regulations designed to protect the public, you've become the monster.

Recall 9/11/2001. How did that atrocity affect your business? What have you done to make sure that if a similar event occurs, you won't get hit as hard the next time?

What are the most likely means by which an internal monster can harm you, that is, someone within the company? Have you initiated sufficient security procedures? Do you remain vigilant about safety issues? Can you protect what makes your company special and successful against attacks by competitors?

As a manager you bear responsibilities for such tasks; you're the closest thing your employees have to a Beowulf. Accept the challenge and think ahead. Imagine even the fearsome and plan against it. No one else will do that for you. In the meantime, encourage your colleagues and employees to expand their education, to learn more about the diversity of the world. In the long run, in a world where terrorism is replacing old notions of conventional war, that's our best bet for destroying the monsters.

Points to Ponder

1. *When was the last time you reviewed security and safety proce-dures essential to your employees or colleagues? Are they still thoroughly up to date?*

2. *Create privately a list of your company's greatest vulnerabilities; develop a (trustworthy) discussion group to evaluate them and enumerate steps to protect against them. If that sounds too James Bondish to you, you haven't been reading a good newspaper.*

13

Dealing with Losses and Failures

The wise one thought
he must have offended against the old law.

(i.e., Know your limitations, but value your freedoms.)

The Idea

Regardless of how good you are at business and at life, eventually you'll have to deal not only with mortality, but also with an array of sorrows, losses, failures. They come to everyone. Beowulf experiences relatively few, at least in the poem, but you and I know that life differs from literature: it envelopes us in good days, average days, bad days, with all the little details of daily existence that most literature can't treat. Otherwise, each book would take a lifetime to read. Literature pleases, teases, teaches, distracts, refracts, imagines, unearths, inspires, inures. But for all its powers and wonders, literature doesn't replace life. If we use literature well, it can help us live better. If failure and sorrow come even to the greatest of literary heroes, certainly we living folk, bound by skin and time, can't escape them either. We can learn a bit from Beowulf, though, about how to deal with sorrows when they come.

"Better to avenge one's friend than mourn overmuch," says Beowulf after Hrothgar has lost his friend Aeschere. For him that's true, but he's young, and even though Grendel has just killed a friend of his, the full weight of mortality probably hasn't hit him yet. And what about us? Many religions prohibit vengeance, though culturally we aim to take it often enough.

We can look at what Beowulf says another way, though: better to act than to mope. Most of us would agree with that. Though some things that happen allow for no compensatory action: we can only mourn lost family and friends, not bring them back. But if we have let opportunities to do something worthwhile go by, we can teach ourselves to take advantage of new ones that arise. When bad things happen that are beyond our control—sometimes they aren't, but often they are—we can decide not to blame ourselves for them and drain our confidence. As *Beowulf* and experience both show, we have a hard time succeeding, even acting at all, without confidence, and the confident person with no greater skill will normally outshine the talented person plagued by self-doubt.

Occasionally we undertake tasks knowing we can't fully *succeed* at them, because coming up short or even failing is better than not trying at all or because the responsibility of the position that we hold requires that we try. Better to have loved and lost than never to have loved at all, goes the old saw. And you don't really know ahead of time that you'll fail—the world has an odd way of turning events unexpectedly.

The book that you want to read but never have will always gnaw at you. The date that you never asked for will turn you maudlin years later. The job that you never applied for will sour your stomach over a bad business lunch. The sport or instrument that you never played will always haunt your dreams. Choices others have made for you, good or bad, have passed away, inflicting their consequences. You must take what freedom you have, the poem suggests, and use it for all its worth.

I remember reading once that the college freshman always has pointless hopes and the senior always has useless regrets. For one thing, if you go to college, when you begin, you can major in anything you want. But year by year you whittle down your choices, until by the time you graduate you've fulfilled a major (or two). But then instead of feeling good about your accomplishment, you inevitably look back on all the choices you could have made, but didn't, and you feel limited, trapped, less free, because of choices you—and everyone else who goes—must make.

Beowulf doesn't say that such feelings are bad. It doesn't comment on feelings at all, but on actions. The feelings are part of life. We feel them, enjoy them or suffer them, and then get back to business.

The Passage

When Beowulf was only seven, his family placed him in the court of King Hrethel, father of Hygelac, where he would be reared by others, according to Germanic custom. They believed that children grew up best in other households than their own, where they would get proper training without either special coddling or the oppressions of doting or over-strict parents. One need not work too hard to imagine the loneliness a child would experience irrespective of the quality of the family who took him in. By the time the poem begins, though Beowulf is still young, his father is already dead, and we learn nothing of his mother or of siblings.

As an adult, a fully fledged hero, in battle Beowulf was unable to prevent the fall of the king whom he'd pledged faithfully to serve with his own life. Later, he couldn't thwart the murder of Hygelac's son, though he avenged it. We get those stories as Beowulf prepares for his final adventure.

Then, as an old man, he must face the dragon knowing he won't survive the encounter.

When he hears of the dragon's attack, for the first time, at least according to what we learn from the poem, he experiences self-doubt: did he do something wrong, he asks himself, that has caused this terrible suffering to be visited upon his people? Has he offended God? He doubts, grieves for his people's losses, and plans vengeance—more than vengeance, he has the obligation to save them from subsequent attacks. The responsibility falls to him alone.

How many of us have asked that question or something like it: why has this happened to me? Did I do something to provoke God to cause me and my family such suffering?

The answer in the poem is that, no, Beowulf had nothing to do with it. But he doesn't know that, and so he asks the question we all would ask.

The important thing: having asked the question, he gets past it. It doesn't freeze his ability to act. Whether he has caused the problem or not, he has the responsibility to try to solve it, and he accepts that responsibility without hesitation.

Armed, and with his hand-picked troop, he strides "humbly" forward, the poet says, to face the dragon. Not even the feeling of his impending mortality will stop him from giving his best effort. He feels sad and ready for death, and yet he musters the vitality to kill the most fearsome of foes.

Of course, like any great leader Beowulf pauses before the battle to give a speech to the followers who will survive him. He recalls many great battles and many great sorrows. He remembers how king Hrethel, father of Hygelac, lost one of his sons, Herebald, shot accidentally with an arrow by his younger brother—the worst of problems for medieval Germanic folk because the death must go unavenged. It's similar, he says, when an old man must watch his son swing on the gallows—an interesting and harrowing comparison. "I wouldn't wield a sword against the worm," he says, "if I knew how else I might honorably grapple with him"—even at the last the desire for a fair fight reigns with him. "I am hardy of heart," he adds, and "I will refrain from boasts," but "I will not retreat one foot from the barrow-guardian"—well, perhaps one little boast. Not long must he wait to encounter the dragon's fire.

The Application

Few of us are heroes, yet each of us experiences both joys and sorrow and suffering. That's a bit of comfort: you're not alone; everyone falls short sometimes, and whatever you feel, someone has felt it before.

When self-doubt creeps in, allow it its time. Consider if doubt makes sense. If it does, get help with the task at hand; if it doesn't, get busy and do your job! The problem isn't feeling the doubt, but being paralyzed by the doubt.

Unless like a dragon you have no sympathy for anyone, you'll feel sorrow as well as doubt—again, a part of life, to be experienced just like joy. The key is not to forget it, but to accept it as genuine, unavoidable, and to press on toward experiences and accomplishments that make suffering bearable and that can displace it with joy.

Some battles you'll win, some you'll lose. Even Muhammad Ali didn't have an unblemished boxing record, yet he still may be, as he said he was, the greatest of all time. I don't know, but I doubt he would exchange his victories for good health now, because to him the battle seems to have been the most important thing—not necessarily true for you and me, but true for him. We pick our battles and live in the midst of them until we win them or lose them. When we win, we celebrate; when we lose, we make certain that we gave our best, and if we survive, we analyze what we learned from the loss and live to battle another day.

These grand—or grandiose—observations apply if in smaller terms to the day-to-day ebb and flood of business practices. Some days your stock will rise, some days fall. Profits will rise and fall. Markets will rise and fall. The price of oil will rise and, well, mostly rise, until the oil runs out not so far ahead. You'll make a sale, you'll lose a sale, you'll make another sale. If you can't sell, don't feel bad: learn to do account books or process orders or use a tool. You don't have to live up to anyone's idea of success, not even your own. You do have to live up to the responsibilities you've accepted—that's what *Beowulf* teaches.

These days a great deal of education focuses on helping children feel good about themselves. What they don't tell you is that the best way to feel good about yourself: work really hard to get really good at something you value and enjoy making the most of the time God has given you in this world.

The Manager's Spotlight

What strategies do you employ regularly to make sure that your people feel confident in their job skills? What have you done recent-

ly to show them that you have confidence in them? Confident and appreciated employees make good employees. You don't even necessarily have to strain the budget to give large raises if you make people feel wanted and needed and as though they're an important part of the team. How many second-string players would happily give up their Super Bowl rings? They too contributed in practices, through occasional play, by providing back-up, and by supporting first-string players.

Not everyone can be a star, but not everyone has to be—neither do you. You must, though, support not only the persons for whom you work, but also the people who work for you. Stroke your ego by building the confidence of your colleagues and by preparing yourself to act in the moment of need. You don't need flamboyance; you need to be steady, ready, and heady. And your employees need to know that you appreciate it when they are, too.

Points to Ponder

1. *For what problems do you feel so prepared that you don't even fear them or worry about them? For what problems should you acquire better preparation?*

2. *Think of a failure that bothers you: could you really have averted it? Every one? Think of a success that pleases you: what would have happened had you not succeeded? Only the most heroic jobs can't permit failure; if you have one of those, what can you do to bolster your confidence so that you approach a task without the possibility of failure clouding your mind?*

14

With a Little Help from His Friends

That was not an easy bargain for anyone to make.

(i.e., Sometimes you'll lose.
Lose courageously and responsibly.)

The Idea

We can complete few complex, worthy tasks on our own, even if we're heroes. Even Beowulf needs a little help in his most dangerous, difficult battle.

Beowulf fights and kills the dragon. Without him we can only guess how much trouble the people would have had from it. J. R. R. Tolkien, famous author of *The Hobbit* and *The Lord of the Rings* and also a *Beowulf* scholar, wrote that we shouldn't even feel too bad for the hero: he dies the best death he could hope for, defeating the worst sort of monster and concluding his life in a mission of which he can feel proud.

As Tolkien says, Beowulf goes out on top. He wins the big one, then exits into the sunset, sacrificing himself for his people. And at his departure he appoints a successor. We can ask little more of a hero than that.

The important point for us in this chapter is that Beowulf does well partly because he receives help in his most critical hour—receives it and accepts it—and that help may make the difference between success and failure.

Some readers say that Beowulf shouldn't fight the dragon at all: he's old; he's a king, no longer a young warrior; he should devise a strategy and bring an army against such a terrifying foe.

But Beowulf knows that no elaborate logistical strategy will work against such an enemy as the dragon. Numbers would only get in the way, and many rather than few or one would die. If he attacks alone, with a small back-up force, he stands the best chance of success, of getting to the dragon and finding its one vulnerable spot. He knows that no one but he has the slightest chance of success: his skills, his temperament, his experience, his commitment prepare him as they prepare no other. But he also knows that even he is unlikely to survive the battle, though he has hope to win if not to live. In this case duty comes foremost: he sees his greatest responsibility as saving his people from immediate, deadly attack rather than protecting himself to govern a people who may not survive without his heroism. Once again we find the theme of the importance of fulfilling one's responsibility.

And that responsibility extends down the chain of command. The man who helps Beowulf destroy the dragon, the only one brave and hardy enough to try, becomes his successor. Those who help best get rewarded most, as they should.

The Passage

Beowulf approaches the battle against the dragon with the thief to guide him to the barrow and with eleven trusted companions to help him support him. Beowulf knows that of all those soldiers only he has the foggiest hope of defeating the dragon. Even if he kills the dragon, he's probably going to be killed as well. The dragon is the most recalcitrant of ancient foes born of the natural world: it has enormous strength, fire, and a nearly impenetrable cover of scales, and it can fly.

Once the battle begins, all but one of Beowulf's followers desert him. Typical, you may say. But the important thing is: one faithful follower, even in the face of death, remains true.

Among those who flee, we're not talking about craven cowards. We're talking about seasoned, trusted soldiers. But they're facing a dragon, an enemy entirely beyond their skill, an enemy that in the blink of an eye can burn them to cinders—nothing they can do about it. In such an instance, very few persons would be able to stand their ground. Very few should even try, and we shouldn't necessarily disparage them for it. Beowulf doesn't. He even tells them, "This isn't your task, nor is it fitting for anyone but for me alone." However, one character does stand, and later he will berate the others for leaving their beloved leader, the man who never left them, at his greatest need. Wiglaf, the one man who stands beside Beowulf to fight the dragon, represents the possibility that in this life we can be true to each other.

Perhaps you don't believe in altruism. But maybe you believe in duty, or love, or practicality.

Wiglaf risks his life to save his leader. We can't be sure that he would do that for just anyone. But he loves his king and has pledged him loyalty, and Beowulf has rewarded that loyalty with gifts, protection, and opportunities for heroism. All the soldiers who go with Beowulf have bound themselves to defend him to the death. Wiglaf fulfills that responsibility.

But his choice has an even greater ramification. Another good
reason for Wiglaf to stay to help his king is that if Beowulf fails,
the Geats have lost their greatest hero, and no one left alive has
the ability to kill the dragon. The people will be left defense-
less and will almost certainly be wiped out.

Self-interest need not conflict with the interests of the greater
population.

Once they reach the barrow, they see steam emerging from the
opening, and Beowulf gives a war-shout to alert the dragon of
their presence. What about stealth? you may ask. It wouldn't
help: heat from the dragon's fire keeps them at too great a
distance to attack. Beowulf crouches behind his shield as
the dragon appears, spewing fire about him. "Fate didn't allot
him success in that battle," the poet says, but that depends on
how we measure success: he dies, but so does his enemy; he
wins his people a load of treasure and salvation from the
monster.

Beowulf strikes the beast a fearsome blow with his sword, but
against the hard scales the weapon fails: it breaks. Beowulf,
who depends on courage, composure, and focus, could never
find a weapon sufficient to his strength or to the difficulty of
his tasks.

As the others flee, Wiglaf calls uselessly for them to stay, then
advances to help his lord, cheering on the great hero as he too
attacks. Dragon-fire burns up Wiglaf's shield, and he leaps
behind Beowulf's for the little protection it offers.

Then as Beowulf tangles with the dragon, the beast having
grasped his neck in its jaws, Wiglaf with his sword strikes far-
ther down on the beast's belly, finding the soft spot, "so that the
fire began to abate." "So should a man be at need," the poet
adds. Beowulf, despite deadly injury, draws his knife and slits

the beast right down the middle, killing it on the spot, and draws himself free of its bite, bleeding and poisoned to death. So with the help of a loyal friend and follower, Beowulf saves his folk from the dragon.

The Application

Most businesspeople, even those who begin small and on their own, with any success at all get to the point where they need support, either from external suppliers or from employees or just from family members in their spare hours. Large companies can only succeed as large companies because of the hard work of many devoted employees at many levels of labor, technical support, sales, and management. Those at the bottom of the reporting chart succeed because those at the top put into place a viable, serviceable system and devote their energies to keeping it running efficiently and effectively. Those at the top succeed only because those at each of the other levels fulfill their tasks with consistency and reliability.

All the people in the organization get along well with a little help from their friends. With continuing problems at any level, an organization will shake and rattle, and without improved relations, it will eventually roll over and die.

A common problem across the realm of manufacturing occurs between labor and management: labor wants more for its time, management wants more for its money. Another occurs in companies dependent on continuing research to sustain old products and develop new ones: those in product development resent those in basic research, believing they don't contribute to the company's real income. Another in the business sector occurs between management or production and sales: the office or lab folk think the salespeople don't push the products hard enough, while the salespeople believe the their colleagues at home don't produce good enough products for them to sell in competitive markets.

The likely solution to all those problems—besides a small company producing a whiz-bang product for a market with no competition—lies in our ability to work as families, as teams, as friends, to remember that we have a much greater hope of success if we accept our responsibilities and vow to fulfill them.

Managers: if you have people in dead-end jobs, do something for them to make them feel appreciated, needed, and understood. If you're in a dead-end job, but you're making fair pay for your work, do your best during your work hours and make your free time fulfilling and your own; if you want more, do your best to find your way to a more rewarding post, either by education or by seeking a position (internal or external) that better suits your skills and aspirations. It's often a hard road, but it's better than fighting dragons.

Meanwhile, give fair work for fair pay. If you face unresponsive management and bad working conditions, you may need to unionize, if you haven't already. In the age of *Beowulf* people and peoples formed troops or alliances to protect themselves, tend their needs, and promote opportunities. That hard old world out there responds better to troops and teams than it does to the lonely individual, even if one happens to be a hero. We love communities, and for good reason: they're safer, more productive, and often more rewarding. As bad as insurance premiums are for employees these days, look into what you'd pay on your own: far worse yet.

Alliances work; exiles, or even heroes, usually fail. Even if they gain individual victories, they lose the larger war. And one war, like Beowulf, we all lose in the end. Seldom can you beat the dragon, and you can hold off mortality only so long.

So live, work, cooperate, and gain your own corner of success, which, by the way, feels better when you can share it with someone else or even a community. Ask the athletes who compete in the Olympics how they feel to have won for their country. Listen to the celebrations in the locker room after the Super Bowl or the Stanley Cup. Success, like a good meal, is better shared with a friend. And mortality goes down more easily with friendship than with loneliness. Ask Ebeneezer Scrooge.

The Manager's Spotlight

Look at your corporate structure. Does it provide fair rewards based on responsibility, productivity, knowledge and experience? If it doesn't, you, as manager, have an obligation to do something to try to improve the system.

The corporate structure has suffered, nearly since its beginnings, from grave imbalances. Greed may be a great motivator, but it's an even greater destroyer. Anyone's success depends on others. Even if you were to make all your products yourself, you'd still depend on your customers, the community you serve. As long as you engage in business, you can't forget your responsibility to them.

Remember, too, that all those you manage depend on you, for a living, for dependability, for advice, for leadership. You need not be a Beowulf to lead well, but you need be the best possible version of yourself. When you succeed, many others succeed; when you fail, many others fail. That's not easy, but it's the way of the world.

Points to Ponder

1. *If you can find them, compare the top salaries and benefit packages in your company to those at the middle and those at the bottom. Are they sufficiently reasonable that persons at each level can maintain their loyalty to the company and perform their duties with a sense of equitability?*

2. *Who are your "Wiglafs"? That is, upon whom can you depend in a pinch? For whom do you serve that function? If you name several (but only) friends and family members, you're pretty lucky, but you may need to acquire more professional alliances if you want to advance in the broader world.*

3. *Given the natural limitations of such a consideration, to what degree do you think of co-workers as though they were "friends" or "family"? Do they think of you or others in your workplace in the same way you do? What can you do to improve the quality of the alliances you have or your company has in the working environment?*

15

The Old Man is Dead

Often many must endure exile for the will of one.

(i.e., Don't impose your problems on others.)

The Idea

Sooner or later you'll have to turn over operations to a new leader. It's inevitable. And it's all right.

So much of the early literature is about mortality. So much of the literature of any time is about mortality.

Some people retire and start a new life. They're happy to get out of the business. Other people have to be carried out: they want to continue working until their last breath. Beowulf is a king; he could get out of that by abdicating, but he'd cause problems for his people if he did that. Who would succeed him? Would he destroy the natural order of things by ignoring divine will and family responsibility? Beowulf is also a hero: in the ancient world, one didn't give up heroism. He dies in the best way an ancient hero can: on the job, fighting a dragon.

That's good for him, but what about for the people who come after him? What should they do?

Beowulf does appoint a successor: Wiglaf. But Wiglaf fears he won't be leader enough to fill his predecessor's mail. The messengers, including Wiglaf himself, all bring the people fearful reports. The dragon is dead, but they have lost the hero who protected them, and the future looks grim.

The key idea here, as we have found so often through *Beowulf*, is *preparation*—along with knowing when to let go, when to take control, and how to cede control.

When at the beginning of the poem we learn about Scyld Scefing, the ideal of a good king, who subdued his neighbors, won tribute, built a strong army, always proved generous, took care of his people, and left an heir, we get a plan for how to run an organization. Now as the poem ends, we find in the case of Beowulf's reign a problem: no clear successor. Beowulf tries to take care of that problem, but even the successor he appoints, Wiglaf, knows that he hasn't enough strength.

Few people want to prepare for their own exit, from business or from life. *Beowulf* teaches us the consequences of failing to provide for a smooth transition after the loss or death of the best and bravest of leaders.

The Passage

Several speeches and two interesting choices develop the idea for this chapter.

As Beowulf sits dying, he speaks to Wiglaf. "Had I a son, an heir to come after me, I would wish to give him my war-gear. I was king for fifty winters, and none of the neighboring tribes dared threaten me. I sought no enemies, broke no oaths, but awaited my apportioned time. I can take pleasure in those deeds now that I have mortal wounds. Go to the dragon's treasure and bring some to show me, so that I may depart this life more gently."

Beowulf knows he is dying and has no personal use for the treasure, but he hopes through it to give the people some recompense for his death.

After he dies, they will bury it with him.

Bad idea. Kind, but bad.

Wiglaf returns from the hoard with an armload of treasure.

"For those treasures I thank the Lord of all, that I was able to win them for my people before my death," Beowulf says, examining his winnings. Then to Wiglaf he says, "I can stay no longer. I have sold my old age. Command the people to make a barrow for me on the headland, so that seafarers will recognize it from far away." Then he gives Wiglaf his helmet, mail-shirt, and neck ring, symbols of his kingship and heroism, and utters his final words: "You are the last of our race. Fate has drawn away all my kinsmen as the Measurer decrees. I must follow them"—and so he dies. The poet comments that as Beowulf lay dead, the dragon lay not far away: "Each had reached the end of a brief (transitory) life."

The soldiers who had fled to the woods creep out to view the carnage. Wiglaf addresses them: "Your lord gave you many treasures and honors and war-gear: he threw them away. He couldn't boast of his war-companions when battle arose. He avenged himself against his killer. Little could I help him, but I stood by my kinsman at need. Now when people far away hear of your cowardice, you'll be deprived of the lands he gave you. Death is better for everyone than a life of reproach."

Wiglaf sends a messenger back to the settlement, and he truly and woefully delivers his message: "the lord of the Geats lies dead with his enemy beside him. Wiglaf keeps watch over both. Now our people can expect war, when Franks and Frisians learn of the fall of our king, nor do I expect peace from the Swedes. . . . Now haste is best, that we take our leader to the funeral pyre, and all the hoard shall go with him."

At the funeral pyre Wiglaf speaks again—the ancient folk loved speeches: "Often must someone, because of the will of another, endure exile. We could not have persuaded the beloved king to forgo the battle: he held to his noble destiny. I brought treasures to him while he was still alive; he commanded me to greet you, bade you build pyre and barrow. . . . Now must fire consume the prince of warriors." They load the pyre with treasures then set it alight. As the fire spills forth its smoke, an unidentified woman sings a funeral lament, a song of loss and sorrow, of invasions, slaughters, humiliation, and captivity to come. They lay the ashes in a barrow, and soldiers ride circles around it. Someone recites a poem praising Beowulf's noble deeds.

Not for those people a happy ending.

The Application

We need not doubt that Beowulf is a good king: the poem ends with the statement that his people said that of the kings of the world he was the mildest, gentlest, kindest to his people, and most eager for fame—that last point not a fault among the people of that age. Even his death is, for him, the best possible— heroes in that society weren't supposed to go quietly, rather in some glorious battle. As king, perhaps Beowulf should, as Wiglaf says, have got someone else to fight the dragon, but that seems not only impossible but also against character. We don't find in the poem anyone asking Beowulf *not* to fight the drag-on—Wiglaf mentions it after the king has died. We may then not be getting an argument about prudence, but a lament: the fact is, sometimes we do say "I wish he'd have done that differently" when we know he couldn't have or even shouldn't have. We simply feel as though something should have gone differently to prevent the sorrowful outcome.

The world, though, must ultimately go that way. Someone must take over for the "old man." Some persons eagerly await that day. Others dread it. Wiglaf dreads it, because he knows that without Beowulf, his people are less formidable, a more tantalizing target for foreign foes. Maybe Beowulf could have left the dragon alone, Wiglaf wonders. But the dragon wouldn't have left the people alone: in the old stories they just don't act that way. We can blame Wiglaf for whining and tell him to get busy and do something. But that would be to deny the respect, appreciation, and love he felt for his king and kins-man.

It isn't wrong to lament the changing of the guard.

But it would be a terrible error to allow the lament to ruin the organization without one's making every effort to keep it alive: we owe that to the generation who built it and gave us our chance to grow and prosper in it. Knowing you can't be a Beowulf doesn't mean you can't try to do the best job you can. Certainly you will not even wish to do your job exactly as the old Beowulf did: you must learn from him or her and find your own way. But try you must, because now the organization depends on you.

Whether or not the Old Guard overindulged—please take care not to, Old Guard—the new must begin where they find them-selves.

We need not see *Beowulf* as a poem about death alone—remember, the medievals liked to read on many levels. We can see it as a poem about change. For us it can serve as a tale of a brave person who through hard work and natural skill inherits a business, builds it into a great success both financially for its own sake and socially for its employees and its community, an organization that operates effectively and ethically, that serves its market without the need to expand too quickly or the desire to eliminate competitors because it serves its own market irreproachably.

No matter how good that owner or manager, eventually he or she must retire and leave the company in trustworthy hands. We have raised this issue before, but now it returns with a twist. In this case no one *can* replace the manager: no available person has the knowledge, the skill, the charisma. What do you do then?

You may sell. But what about the employees? What about customers and business allies and others in the community who depend on your business? In *Beowulf* we get the sense that foreign invaders will arrive to take over Geatland. That wouldn't be so bad except that they'll probably kill or enslave the inhabitants. Maybe you'll look for a "white knight" to take over your company: better get a good one, and that's not easy, else you're likely to see your people fired, your resources scattered, and your community alienated—a business is always part of a community.

No one can replace the "old man," but we need a heroic effort from Wiglaf. Who knows what he can accomplish if he makes the effort? He must make the effort to reinvision the future of the company: what can we do? what can't we do? what help do we need, and what can we get? if we have no choice but to dissolve, how can we do our best to take care of all concerned?

Then again maybe you don't have to sell, dismantle, or close the company. Maybe you need to take it in a new direction. Or maybe you just need to be Wiglaf long enough to grow into Beowulf and run the company with the same verve and elan the old man did.

Sometimes you have to take charge even if you don't want to. That's showing respect, not disrespect, for those you follow and what they accomplished. Often the best leader is the one who has the knowledge and commitment, but doesn't want to lead. That's when the time has come for heroism. The person who does want to lead may not be trustworthy—we have to do our best in the rough, often rotten world to learn to discern the difference between the person who leads to serve and the one who leads to hoard.

Beowulf's followers fail him, but it may not have made much difference had they not. Wiglaf doesn't fail, at least not yet, and he won't go down without a fight.

Beowulf's one error, that he hasn't prepared Wiglaf well enough for him to be confident, or that he hasn't had a child so exactly like him to be able to fill his heroic boots, occurs all too often in the world. It happens not necessarily because of pride—though we have many leaders who say, no one will come along who's as good as I am; the world is getting worse every year.

Sometimes circumstances do decline, either through our errors or through no particular fault on anyone's part. We age, and the world changes. If you have accomplished something worth preserving—and nearly any successful organization is worth that effort—do your best to prepare your Wiglaf to take your place. Keep your records in order, your training programs fair and intense, and abandon ego enough to know that nobody is really a Beowulf: out there is somebody who can do your job, preserve what you've won, and make things better. Part of your job is to find such people and train them, then let the quality show itself in battle.

The Manager's Spotlight

Where would you be tomorrow if your boss or CEO retired today? How would those who depend on you react, and how could you help to make the transition to new leadership smooth and successful?

You never know when the dragon will appear. Too many of us blunder along from day to day assuming things will work tomorrow just exactly as they do today—history has recorded the fall of millions of people who thought that way.

If your boss has too tight a hold on his or her job to help you learn how to do it, you need to find subtle ways to learn as much as you can anyway. Who knows how loyal your superiors really are to the company and its customers and employees? They may jump at the next opportunity to fall before them and leave the job for what they believe to be a better opportunity. But then, so may you. You must be a Wiglaf, whether or not you have the potential ever to be a Beowulf.

If your boss behaves immorally or unethically, you don't have an obligation to defend him or her. You do have an obligation, Beowulf suggests, to the people who depend on you and the community who depend on your company. You must be loyal to what your employer should be.

Points to Ponder

1. *How well do you know your boss's job? How well do your subordinates (or clients or allies or students) know your job?*

2. *To what degree do you feel loyal to your organization? Think about why you feel that way, and try to enumerate the reasons.*

3. *Think about the traits we've discussed that best characterize Beowulf and Wiglaf: whom do you know who best exhibits comparable versions of those traits? To what degree do they contribute to those persons' success?*

16

The Problem with Treasure

Treasure can easily overcome anyone—
take heed if you will.

(i.e., Greed, like speed, can kill.)

The Idea

Regardless of other reasons, personal, moral, professional, nearly every one of us works for money. Most of us dream at one time or another about having a lot of it, about what a really significant amount of wealth could do for us and our families.

Beowulf extols the value of wealth: for *giving*. The important thing is that we not get obsessed with wealth for its own sake. The dragons who hoard wealth represent an insidious plague, a disease.

Ever since human beings invented money, we've enjoyed talking and writing about it almost as much as acquiring and spending it. Look at the literature of Shakespeare's time, about seven centuries after *Beowulf* and four before our own. It explores all the old problems, the "Seven Deadly Sins," but more and more writers turned their attention to the overwhelming sin of the growing modern age: greed, or cupidity: love of money not for the good it can help us do, but for its own sake.

Some people will even tell you greed is a good thing, that it motivates people, that without it no one would really work very hard. Look, they'll say, at communist countries: people work only as hard as they have to, and so they always fail to improve or advance and their companies and countries fall apart. That's sometimes true and sometimes not, as it is in most places, but it misses the point that *Beowulf* makes on this very subject: if you work and make money for the sake of greed, to hoard and make more, you're on your way to becoming a dragon, if you haven't done so already—you yourself are the disease, a danger to your country.

You may think, better to be the dragon than to be eaten by the dragon. *Beowulf* says, not so. We could make religious arguments against greed, of course, but to do that correctly we'd need the help of a friendly neighborhood theologian. *Beowulf* hints at religious reasons, but it deals with this issue in an immediate and eminently "practical" way.

If you make wealth your target, you become the target of others who target wealth. If you hoard it, you alienate all the people most likely to help defend you when you need them. As Beowulf shows us, they may fail you anyway. But if your followers cling to you only because they hope you'll allow a few castoff drops to trickle down to them, they'll surely abandon you even if they get their trickle: you've made them grovel for next to nothing, reduced their humanity to begging for the merest sustenance. If they're starving, they may praise you for the moment. When they recover and learn what you've done, they'll hate you forever.

If you abuse your wealth, every Beowulf, as well as everyone who suffers from your abuse, will be your enemy; if you display it to gratify ego, every two-bit hustler will try to fleece you.

Beowulf says, it's good to have wealth, but be wary of where and how you get it. If it's yours, use it well. If it isn't, you'll spend your strength defending it, and it won't be worth the trouble.

The Passage

As Beowulf waits outside, dying, Wiglaf follows his king's request and hurries inside the dragon's barrow to get a look at the treasure and bring some for Beowulf to see.

Jewels, gold, rings, and war gear, but rusty helmets, mail-shirts, and cups that have corroded, lacking tending and polishing perhaps for centuries: Wiglaf finds all the items that for his culture had such great value either in practical use or as symbols of one's worth or as gifts for building alliances, and briefly he gives in to the treasure's fascination. Who wouldn't? Buried treasure!

"Treasure, gold buried in the ground, can easily overcome anyone of the human race: heed this he who will," warns the narrator.

The poet wants to make quite clear that temptations occur all the time, and no one among us is so strong as to be entirely above them. Even when his beloved king is drawing his last breaths, Wiglaf, the faithful one, is still so drawn to the treasures that he pauses over them—briefly, but a pause nonetheless.

Then again, Beowulf, too, is thinking about the hoard.

As his last deed, Beowulf kills the dragon to protect his people and win the treasure hoard. As we discussed in the last chapter, then, when they bury his ashes, they bury the treasure with him.

What he's won with his life, they throw away.

Why do they do it? Partly they use the treasure to honor their dead king. Partly, they realize they haven't earned it. Partly, they probably sense that, since it comes from a dragon's hoard, it's probably cursed anyway, and the poet suggests that's right.

Having the treasure would only remind them that they don't deserve it: when their hero won it, they failed him.

We need not worry too much about the rusty armor and weapons Wiglaf finds in the barrow: someone can always clean and polish them, though their presence returns us to the theme that material things and even memories eventually pass away. The bigger problem in this passage is the weaponry rusting in the sheathes of those who failed their leader at need.

They probably couldn't have helped. But they'll always wish that they'd tried.

The Application

In that little line, "heed this [message] he who will," the poet emphasizes the point of this chapter: treasure (or wealth) can bring about good, or it can cause harm.

Temptation greets us all, and in a weak moment anyone may give in—all the more reason to steel ourselves against it.

We're not talking about inconsequential indulgences: a scoop of ice-cream after dinner, an extra hour's sleep on a Saturday, a bit of shopping when you're feeling low. The poem doesn't berate us for being human. We're talking about when temptations get in the way of our responsibilities to one another, not just as employees or colleagues, but as persons.

If a heroic figure such as Wiglaf can get distracted in the moment of fulfilling his dying king's request, how much more easily can we find our attention turned aside from acts of kindness, courtesy, or professionalism that make life easier and better for others and that help us rise above our limitations to become better persons.

Often the better we are, the happier we are—and that means either more skilled in our ventures or just better as human beings.

The way to make yourself unhappy, the poem suggests, is to identify yourself with your wealth. Whether you keep it or lose it, you've lost yourself in it. Lose yourself in things material or in any action you know to be wrong, and you've lost your ability to believe in anything, because you no longer have anything to believe *with*. You've given up the one thing you really had.

So the people give up the treasure they've acquired but can't accept as theirs, having lost the true treasure they already had: their belief in themselves and their leader's belief in them. Wiglaf feels the greatest sadness of the lot, yet in the long run he will be the happiest: he tried to do his best, and with only the briefest pause, he rejects temptation and remains true to himself, his lord, and his duty.

Such grand problems may not apply to you on your job. The poet says, simply, "heed this he who will." No message applies at all times to all persons in all cases. Poems give us a way or several ways among many of looking at achievements or at problems. We need not feel it perilous to set them aside as inapplicable. Yet we may find that some of them provide insight, knowledge, and strength if we remember them.

They remind us of what's good and bad about joy and what helps us avoid or deal with sorrow. They exemplify what's good and bad about treasure.

Heed who will.

The Manager's Spotlight

Take care with employees who work with you for one reason only: money. That doesn't mean you should despise or even dislike or fail to respect them. Most of us must earn a living. But place your trust in those persons who work for something more as well: for family, for self-respect, to contribute, because they believe in your organization. They're much more likely to support you in hard times.

If you find yourself working purely for the money, you may need to make a change, either in your attitude or in your job, or maybe in your life or in yourself. Life is too short and takes too much struggle for you to spend so much time and effort only for money. You may work because you must, to support a family: that makes your efforts both necessary and praiseworthy. But at some point, if and when you've met your responsibilities, you'll need to examine what you're doing and why, so you can consider how you want to spend the remainder of your precious, irreplaceable days.

Points to Ponder

1. *What "treasures" have you acquired through work and through living? Which have the most value to you? Why?*

2. *Make a list of the treasures — other than wages and benefits — that you acquire through your current job. What makes them important to you?*

3. *What treasure are those who work with or for you acquiring? Think about whether or not you know what really matters to your colleagues and employees; if you don't know, why not?*

17

How to Be a Hero

I thank the lord of all I was able to win that for my people.

(i.e., Appreciate life and your accomplishments.)

The Idea

In an excellent movie from 1981 called *Chariots of Fire*, the new freshmen at Caius College, Cambridge, have gathered, only a couple years after the end of World War I, for their introductory formal dinner. The Master of the College, whom we'd call Professor or Dean or Chair, addresses them with an inspirational speech. He concludes by asking that each student find where his (sorry, all males then) true chance for greatness lies, then let nothing deter him from pursuing it.

Think of that: not your chance for success; not your chance for wealth; not even your chance for happiness; your chance for *greatness*.

He's asking them to become heroes.

That's an awfully tall order, considering that he's probably not even a hero himself.

What he is doesn't matter. What he's attempted makes all the difference, and that's the message he wants to communicate to the new students. Most people, if they aim at all, cease their efforts at mediocrity. They lack the confidence or drain themselves of the energy they need to become outstanding in their activities. The Professor's suggesting that if you want to be happy and successful (from which wealth may or may not come), you have to find your truest talents and pursue them with all the vigor and good grace you have in you. Happiness comes in the process, the attempt; success *is* the attempt.

That's true if you're doing something you choose, something you enjoy. Not everyone has that luxury. For thousands of years people found themselves enslaved, literally or figuratively, to their jobs.

If you're stuck in your job now, you may still try to do the best work you can, but you probably must find your satisfaction, your greatness, elsewhere: in love of your family or friends, in a sport or activity you love, in books or conversations or prayers that give you hope.

If you're not stuck in a job, but work at it because you choose it, even if it has less than ideal range, creativity, or responsibility, you can become great at it. You'll live more happily as you try. And, if your company does better because of it, your greatness will help other people prosper as well.

Beowulf finds his true self and his true pleasure in acts of heroism. He turns down kingship until he must accept it, but even then he doesn't abandon his heroic nature. Though he dies as a result of battle, and his death leaves his people open to likely attack, he has done all he can both for them and to fulfill himself. He sets an example of ideal heroism—too much for anyone to achieve, but perfect to inspire.

That's all you can do, too. But your best takes a true commitment. The greater your talent, the greater the responsibility and the longer the road to achievement. Then again, the more fully you fulfill that talent, the greater your happiness.

That's not to say that each of us should pursue each talent to the point of utter exhaustion. Nor does it mean that if you pursue a talent honestly, vigorously, completely, you'll necessarily gain victory, wealth, and praise from it.

Beowulf doesn't teach a pollyanna notion that everybody is a hero, that we're wonderful just for being, or even that each of us has heroism in us. It suggests, though, that, as the Caius College professor says, if we rejoice in the pursuit of our true talents and fix ourselves on greatness through them, we will reach, have reached, the greatest success a person can hope for, and we're likely to find the greatest happiness available to us within the limitations of our life's circumstances.

We don't even get to choose our talents, though we may choose among our talents. The person who wants desperately to be a pro quarterback may have much greater talents in accountancy; the person who wants to be a famous ballet dancer may have the perfect mind for engineering; the person who wants to climb Mt. Everest and sound the Marianas Trench may have the perfect skills to teach school.

Not even the best soldiers in Hrothgar's court have the ability to stop Grendel. Beowulf shows no desire to be king. We often have our opportunities taken from us or thrust upon us by politics, economics, birth, or chance.

The Passage

Earlier in the poem we learn that in childhood Beowulf was what the Norse folk called a "coalbiter," someone who doesn't accomplish much because he doesn't *try* much. A coalbiter sits by the fire to stay warm, close enough to bite the fuel in the grate. His people expected little of him. But he finds his talent and pursues it with conviction and courage.

When he grew, he took on the greatest challenges and responsibilities of his time. In the poem he defeats and destroys the terrible monsters his world can align against him, reigns successfully as king for fifty years, avenging those who died before him and bringing peace to his country until his death. He appoints Wiglaf, the best leader he can find, to take his place. Beyond that, others must assume leadership, learning from him and finding their own way.

He dies loved and honored, having completed his most difficult and important task, and his people grant him a glorious funeral. To them he was the mildest, gentlest, and kindest of kings, and among heroes the most eager for fame, a fame he wins indeed.

Beowulf doesn't escape failure, nor does each victory come with easy perfection. Having eliminated the monsters that trouble the Danes—not without difficulty against the she-beast—he can't prevent the subsequent problems that arrive for the ruling family. He can't prevent the death of King Hygelac in battle nor the murder of Hygelac's son, though he avenges them. He kills the dragon, but receives his death wound, failing to have raised an heir of abilities matching his own, someone who could have extended the peace that he brought to Geatland.

Heroism doesn't imply perfection. It requires ability, effort, application, courage, sacrifice, and striving for greatness, not of place, but in accomplishment.

What happens to Beowulf when he dies? The poem doesn't say explicitly; it gives us an ambiguous image. As his pyre burns and a woman sings a lament, "Heaven swallowed the smoke." Does that mean that Beowulf achieves salvation in the Christian sense, that his spirit rises to Heaven, or does it mean that the body dissolves into smoke that dissipates into a disinterested sky, or does it imply that the heathen soul, like the body, burns in Hell below? Readers must answer that question for themselves. If to you the only heroic success is Salvation, you may dislike the ambiguity created by the poet's use of an image rather than a clear statement of Beowulf's end. The poem, though copied down by a Christian hand, may well have been originally composed by someone either not Christian or converting to Christianity or speaking to an audience part Christian, part non-Christian, and so unwilling to offend either group.

For this chapter we may simply say that Beowulf dies a hero, having fulfilled beyond anyone's hope his incredible abilities, having done all he could for his people, and having set an example of courage and commitment to action.

That's a pretty good legacy.

The Application

No one expects you, unless you're a trained fire fighter, to rush into a burning building to save someone there. No one expects you, unless you're a trained police officer, to comb Metropolis' streets fighting crime. No one expects you, unless you're a trained surgeon, to perform an emergency operation on a critically injured patient. No one expects you, unless you're an experienced and masterful CPA, to set right the accounts of an enormous company troubled by criminally doctored books.

You don't have everyone's talents; you have your talents. You have no obligation to use them. They're gifts, whether of God or nature or chance is a matter of belief.

But to take the talents you have, find those that have the most potential to fulfill you as a person and benefit your family and community: that's how to be a hero, according to *Beowulf* or almost any other source you can find.

You may not make it. Few people do. But that, says the poem, is the accomplishment worth striving for. It does the most good and provides hope of the most lasting fame.

Perhaps you don't want fame. I don't blame you. It seems to do most people who live with it more harm than good. On the other hand, most of us would like to be remembered kindly and honorably when we're gone, at least by our families if not by the world at large.

Beyond fame, heroism leads to the great deeds, whether works of art, cures for diseases, space travel, greater safety for a country or community, or greater wisdom for the world. Gandhi never struck a blow, nor did Martin Luther King or Mother Theresa, but the heroism of each has brought the world a step toward kindness and peace.

We have a long way to go, and we need you.

In business heroism can mean working hard on that new product, creating new, appropriate, and productive streams of revenue, or designing a simpler, safer, faster production line, but it can also mean improving the working conditions or health plan for your employees, refusing to participate in processes that destroy the environment, or helping solve disputes between management and labor. It means making the effort to make a difference, to make the workplace and community better, and not only for your own sake. It means extending your consciousness outside yourself, as athletes do when they perform for their countries.

Not everyone can accomplish it, but everyone can admire, appreciate, and reward it in others, and when the opportunity arises, we may accept the challenges to heroic effort that come our way and gain confidence in ourselves for attempting them.

While not everyone has heroic strength or courage or wisdom, if we read *Beowulf* symbolically, it does suggest that heroism resides in the great effort of will or spirit: the parent who works two jobs to send her children to college; the intern who works ridiculously long hours to learn the art and discipline as well as the science of medicine; the soldier who returns to the battlefield to save a fallen comrade; the cleric who serves a difficult, underprivileged congregation; the teacher who insists on helping the lost student persist or the talented student excel; the person who tolerates the pain and disgust that go with cleaning up after the messes of all sorts that thoughtless persons leave behind them.

Beowulf continues to believe in heroism and self-sacrifice and honor and glory long into what for his time would be amazing old age. It's a hard thing to ask, with the world full of trouble and horror and suffering, that we continue to believe in the intrinsic value of a good day's work. But we can do it.

We can do it.

We need not be Beowulf; we need only gain confidence in and appreciation for whatever version of Beowulf lives in us.

The Manager's Spotlight

We can easily get either cynical or sentimental about heroism. You can't really expect it of yourself or others, but you can appreciate and reward it when you find it. What a shame if one of your employees really makes a heroic effort, then no one commends, rewards, of even notices him or her for it. Some people will even resent such deeds, out of envy or spite. Allowing that sort of attitude poisons the workplace. You must set an example of professional, honorable behavior. Demanding it of yourself may or may not help you get it from others—human beings are unpredictable that way—but it will increase your confidence in and appreciation for yourself as manager.

Managing is about leading, keeping things in order, apportioning, sharing, and taking responsibility. Allow yourself the privilege of accepting those duties toward your subordinates and desiring—if not always expecting—them of your superiors.

Points to Ponder

1. *What heroic efforts have you witnessed? Why do you remember them? Have you ever made one—or more?*

2. *Who in your workplace seems most heroic? What traits give you that impression? Can you—and should you—encourage those traits in your co-workers?*

3. *Observe persons who succeed seemingly without heroic efforts or traits; how do they do it? What can you learn from them,*

behaviors either to follow or avoid? Remember: not every hero is a role model.

18

Reviewing the Whole: And the Value of the Parts

He was the mildest, gentlest, kindest, most eager for fame.

(i.e., Be good. Live well.)

The Idea

We've now completed a tour of duty through the epic poem *Beowulf*. Like most experiences, it has its share of interesting and memorable parts, but the impact of the whole somehow adds up to more than those parts. So let's go back and look at what the whole of the story accomplishes and how the parts contribute to what the whole epic teaches us.

Think of an impressive wild, natural scene: Niagara Falls, the Grand Canyon, a vista in the Rocky Mountains: the experience of each landscape adds up to far more than falling water, a large hole in the ground, or a slope with a few trees on it. Any good work of art has the same effect: it will stay with you in memory, but it also seems to become a part of your flesh and bones. It can provide pleasure years later as you remember its magnitude and beauty.

A person's career is rather like that: a sum of parts, but more than the parts alone or together. Individual experiences do more than just add up: they resonate with one another, and as we learn and grow, they take on layers of significance. Each of us plays more than one role, as a professional, a family member, a friend, a contributor to a community. Our experiences change how we respond to the world in each of those roles.

Are you the version of yourself that your parents see, that your spouse sees, that your friends see, that your co-workers see, that you see? Are you the version of yourself you were when you were five years old, or sixteen years old, or twenty-one, or thirty-five—which is the real you?

The whole evolves through the experience of the parts, yet part of us remains discrete from any particular experience and untouchable to all of them, whether one explains that part by spirituality or DNA or ego/id/superego or any other pattern we may observe or devise.

Similarly, a company is more than the sum of its parts, more than just its employees and resources and stockholders. Whether a company loses a CEO or a personnel officer or an engineer or a manual laborer, that loss changes the company in more and greater ways than just the loss of a part in a machine. The human dynamic changes, whether for the worse or the better, and the loss takes an adjustment. Hiring a new person means more than adding a part to a machine, and the new hire will change the working environment in unexpected ways.

As a piece of literature, art, or music may have an impact on us for our whole lives or may make a minimal impression and then fade from memory, every person we add to an organization and every experience we add to the panoply of our lives changes us at least a little and has the potential to alter our perspectives entirely.

If we appreciate the potential influence of any choice that we make—personnel or personal—we will attend more carefully to the parts so that they help produce a better whole, and we will aim to keep the whole healthy so best to maintain and appreciate the parts.

The Passage

Here we address the impact of *Beowulf* as a whole. Our culture has come to use the word *epic* as an adjective, as in an "epic novel" or "film epic" or "epic experience," by which we normally mean something big, important, and moving. Originally the word was just a name for a kind of literature, a long poem that tells a serious story and addresses an idea, event, or issue significant to a people.

Either use applies to *Beowulf*. Though some scholars say it's too short to be classed with the poems of Homer and Virgil, like the great epics of Greece and Rome it has an impact on the reader beyond just its brief adventures. Like a rewarding relationship, or a great conversation, or an unexpected act of kindness, the more you linger over its details, the more you see, the more you enjoy, and the more you appreciate its power.

Some people see *Beowulf* as having two parts: the battles with the Grendel-kin and the battle with the dragon. Some see it as having three parts: the three monster battles. Some see it as a series of events evolving toward the greatest battle we all face and lose in the end, the one against death. Some see it as a series of battles punctuated by digressions that teach us about what makes the battle scenes important—that is, they help us understand why we should see *Beowulf* as more than just a comic-book-style adventure story, as one scholar put it, a thumping good tale of our pagan forebears. It's more than that mostly because when we're done reading *Beowulf*, it *feels* like more than that. It leaves readers thinking about what it means and about why it affects us so much.

If perhaps you've read *Beowulf* and didn't get anything from it, either you read a bad translation, or you missed what it says, or you didn't get the proper help to read it closely. Like most experiences in life, you must apply some effort to gain rewards from a task. If you've read it carefully and didn't *like* it, that's another matter: as the Romans said, *de gustibus non est disputandem*—there's no disputing matters of taste, and some people just don't like stories about battles. But then we don't always like every task from which we gain understanding or contribute to a greater cause—that's why we call a job *work* and not *play*.

Careful reading and analysis does contribute to the "greater cause," in that through study we can learn to help one another get better. It makes us smarter: better able to understand human beings past and present and to work through, appreciate, and integrate others' thoughts and experiences into our own methods for problem-solving. And *Beowulf* isn't strictly about battles, at least not in the human vs. monster sense. Remember how we discussed the layering of medieval poems. It's about all the issues we've addressed together so far and all those we'll address in the coming chapter—and, I suspect, many more besides. I find something new every time I reread it—that's one way to determine the greatness of a work of art.

For now we can say that the individual parts of *Beowulf* offer a number of interesting ideas or lessons and that the poem as a whole, despite its relative brevity, has the power to stimulate thoughts and emotions that can move us to examine how we live and how we think about life and work. The hero does his work dutifully, but also for the most part joyfully: he lives completely in the acts of his choices, challenges, and adventures. That's among the most important lessons of Zen Buddhism, too: live fully in the moment. Beowulf thinks and feels, but he also acts. He embraces the process of living according to the gifts instilled in him by the Divine spark. Without intruding unnecessarily on the lives of others—except where they would do murder and cause mayhem—he throws himself into the process of fulfilling his talents; without complaint he throws himself equally into fulfilling his responsibility to others. He models for us not just the heroic, but the self-fulfilling human life, the life well and fully lived, in the parts and in the whole.

The Application

Few details are too small to deserve our attention. Often we blunder about, ignoring most of what we encounter in a day. But as the old saying goes, life is in the details. Here we may add to that point: our lives add up to more than the details that comprise them, though only if we appreciate and employ the details as we go. They're all we have from which to build a life that feels whole and satisfying. From details we can build principles, and principles help us guide our lives in meaningful ways.

There's something appealing, heroic, and even soothing about a job well done and a life well lived. Think about how you feel after completing an arduous task. You may feel enlivened or exhausted, but either way you feel a sense of connectedness and satisfaction. Even if no one else is present to share the joy of completion with you—perhaps you work largely alone—when you finish a job you have left behind a memento of your own existence and accomplishment, something that other people can use and value. They may not know you've done it, but you'll know. Think of how many persons contribute to the details of your daily life, in the clothes you wear, the food you eat, the building in which you work or sleep, the society that dashes about you—you'll know very few of them, but nonetheless they've contributed something to the fabric of your life.

When you do your job, you contribute to their lives as well. It's a mutual gift and a mutual responsibility.

The persons for whom you work owe you a sense of the value of your contribution to the organization as a whole.   In exchange, you owe them good work for as long as you wish to remain with the organization.

You are a part of the organization, but as a human being you are more than a part and more than just a member of an organization: you belong as well to yourself, your family, your community, your world. To succeed in life you must find a way to balance those memberships and honor them all, and no one has the right to attempt to reduce you to less than what you are, a whole human being with levels of thought and feeling and a variety of affiliations, responsibilities, and potentials.

If you are a manager, you owe that consideration to each employee. As an employee, you must remember, too, that the company doesn't exist for you alone. Any company, any project, amounts to more than the sum of individual contributions. Responsibilities of the group as a whole, and the achievements of the group as a whole, represent something beyond the individual's capacity. When you accept employment, you have made a commitment to that greater level of achievement that comes from a community's success.

The key is balance. We err when we ask others to give up their humanity, but we err when we fail to move ourselves or encourage others to fulfill our responsibilities to those groups of which we constitute an essential part.

As with Beowulf, we too have our battles that accumulate over the years, our heroic efforts along with our moments thinking and warming ourselves at the coal stove, our victories along with our failures. Personally and professionally, if we heed and perfect the details from the foundation we lay to the bricks and mortar that we stack upon it, with a little luck we can build of this life something worth experiencing and remembering, something that will leave behind a source of comfort and power for those who come after us.

The Manager's Spotlight

This chapter aims to encourage a blend between analytical and holistic thinking. You must be able to do both to build successes. You must be able to encourage individual employees' competence and confidence in their particular details while seeing the bigger picture yourself and communicating it to them when you can. Everyone likes to know where he or she fits into the grand scheme; if you can help your charges understand, appreciate, and commit themselves to that, you're halfway to success.

Nearly everyone likes to be part of the big picture—few persons are really complete loners. Affiliation does matter, and people take it seriously if their leaders give them reason to do so. Look at how people cheer for sports teams, often without knowing a single player: we feel honored and enlivened through the sense of affiliation with excellence, accomplishment, or even just effort. Sometimes a sense of belonging or a vague connection is enough—look at how many fans remain loyal even to losing teams.

Your task is to strengthen that sense of affiliation and strengthen the

*commitment to details without ever losing sight of the whole pic-
ture—a lot to ask, but then as a manager you have accepted the role
of leadership. And leadership requires equal appreciation for—and
occasional fixation on—both.*

Points to Ponder

1. *Explain as exactly as you can your contribution to the larger mission of your organization as a whole. Explain your boss's as well.*

2. *What details of your job do you find most appealing? Which do
you find least appealing? If you look at less appealing elements
as essential to the organization as a whole, does that help you
complete them more fully and comfortably? If not, discuss with
a colleague strategies for making them, if not pleasant, at least
tolerable.*

3. *In an old Zen story a student asks a master to define happiness.
The master says, "Grandparent dies, parent dies, child dies." The
student, upset, asks how so much death can cause happiness. The
master replies that, since mortality is general, the best we can
hope for is that our own experience follows the course of nature.
Tragedy occurs when things happen out of order rather than in
proper order, when child dies before parent or parent before
grandparent. Depressing story, but true enough! In another
story with a similar meaning, the student asks the same question.
The master replies, "Have you eaten?" When the student
assents, the master says, "Then you'd better wash your bowl."
Explain the zen master's answer in terms of "the part and the
whole."*

19

The Power of Digressions

Seldom will the death-spear rest, though the bride be good.

(i.e., Life is in the details.)

The Idea

If life is in the details, it's also in the digressions.

Beowulf, as I've mentioned, has quite a number of what some readers call digressions, little stories that stray from the central plot of the poem. But each one strays for a reason; each provides a little piece of wisdom that helps us understand either what the poem means or some other important facet of the world from which the poem comes.

Our contemporary world differs quite a lot from the early medieval world of *Beowulf*, but people remain much the same. With people, as Ecclesiastes says, there's nothing really new under the sun. We still work for a living, fall in love, feel happy or tired or angry or confused or disgusted, try to understand what life is all about and how we fit into it.

The digressions in *Beowulf* can still help us better understand some of those problems.

They also show us how much of the act and process of living occurs not in the "main plot," what someone else would see as the general course of our lives, but in the little, almost uneventful but often wonderful day-to-day twists and turns of feeling or experience that fill us out as complete human beings—to borrow a term from the previous chapter, in the details.

This chapter will exhume several different ideas from different spots in the text. We'll look more closely at the most important digressions in *Beowulf* and consider what they have to say to us, how they can help us live better, more successful lives.

If we read them carefully, those passages tend to remind us of things we've already learned, but that we easily forget, not especially truths about grand notions like heroism, but observations about actions that can make our lives a little more pleasant or a lot more horrible. They give us examples of what happens when we do our duty well or when we do it poorly or fail in it altogether or simply don't prepare for the future. They make *Beowulf* more a poem of ideas rather than just an adventure tale (not that there's anything wrong with a good adventure tale). Interestingly enough, the little truths of *Beowulf*'s time apply pretty well to some of the problems of our own time or of any time, because they tend to comment on the good and ill of human nature, the interplay of which constantly affects the unfolding of professional as well as personal life.

And remember: new ideas, the really good ones, always begin as digressions.

The Passage

Among the passages for this chapter, we'll take a new look at some we've considered in previous chapters to expand on what else we can learn from them, and we'll also look at a couple of minor incidents that we haven't yet discussed. Our aim is to move toward more of the gems of wisdom that characterize the poem and that show the continuity of human existence that effects so much of how we work and play.

The fact that the poem begins with a digression is instructive: it suggests that the poet finds the digressions just as important as the plot in terms of communicating ideas.

The synopsis of the life and death of King Scyld Scefing warns us that while the poem will deal with noble persons and noble deeds, none of us escapes mortality. But it shows more than that: it gives, as we detailed in an earlier chapter, a blueprint for a successful leader; it shows us the importance of knowing and understanding the past and valuing those who came before us; it explains the value of family and of strength in international relations; it teaches us the value of charity. If the Danes hadn't taken care of the destitute child, he wouldn't have grown up to become their most significant leader. Even if we consider him mythical, his story sets the standard for all rulers to come, establishing his people as noble and worthy of respect. No one can live up to a myth, but anyone may try.

Later, as a contrast to Scyld, after Beowulf's victory over Grendel, Hrothgar's court poet not only praises Beowulf's deeds, but also reminds his audience of Heremod, the exemplar of a bad king (as Modthrytho, the bad queen, contrasts with Hrothgar's good queen, Wealhtheow), one who lost his courage, caused nothing but grief to his people, and abandoned generosity in favor of his own greed. Paired with Heremod's story is that of Sigemund, who slew giants and gained great fame by killing a dragon, daring its fire to win a vast treasure. Of course, your English teacher will tell you that Sigemund serves in the poem to foreshadow Beowulf's later battle with the dragon, but for our purposes the elder hero does more than that: he shows that Beowulf, while unusual, isn't unique.

Hrothgar's court poet also recites the lay of Hildeburh and Finn, which we've discussed before as well. In its particular place in the poem, this story shows what a difficult time people have keeping the peace, even when they've plainly stated that as their goal and taken steps to assure it. Again this story foreshadows more battle ahead for Beowulf, but more importantly for us it shows the sorrows of those persons on whom we impose roles and whom we expect to assume those roles without question or relief and often without hope of success. Hildeburh's family have her married to an enemy to try to end a blood-feud, but the two tribes don't want to stop feuding, and they don't. Hildeburh has little hope of success though she has no choice but to accept the duty of trying. Among all those who suffer from the feud, she suffers most, because she loses family on both sides. She does her duty, but fails through no fault of her own, and yet she bears the brunt of the burden for others' failure.

When Beowulf returns home, he tells Hygelac of all his adventures in Denmark—his report is with respect to the whole poem a digression of sorts, since it recounts what we already know rather than advancing the story. Beowulf allows himself a couple personal digressions as he recounts details of Hrothgar's court and his battles with the monsters. First he mentions Hrothgar's daughter, Freawaru, whom her father has promised to Ingeld, prince of the Heathobards, to end a feud between the two peoples. He gives a somewhat lengthy speculative account of what's likely to happen at the wedding, how some old soldier will point out to a young one that one of the visitors is wearing a sword that should belong to him rather than the bearer, thus inciting the young man to violence on an occasion that should promote peace and celebration. Fighting begins anew, and the prince's love for his new princess cools even before time has the chance to erode it.

That passage of course reinforces what we learned in the digression about Hildeburh—the problem of imposing an impossible role on another person's life—but it also suggests some other points as well. Maybe Beowulf felt that, through his heroic deeds, he had earned the princess as his own bride, only to have his hopes dashed by a previously arranged marriage. Hrothgar gives Beowulf excellent gifts, but not that one. He does say that he thinks of Beowulf as though he were his son, but he gives no hint of making him son-in-law. Nor should Beowulf expect that: he goes to Denmark for another purpose and achieves that purpose: he repays a debt, helps a beleaguered people, and wins fame and glory. The passage also shows Beowulf's awareness of human weakness, indicating that he looks at situations realistically, not romantically—a necessary trait for a successful warrior.

In another digression known as the "Lay of the Last Survivor," when the thief steals the cup from the dragon's hoard, the poet returns to the original burying of the hoard. Explaining how death had taken all but one man, the last of his tribe, the poet improvises a speech such a man might have made. "Hold now, you earth, since heroes cannot, the treasures of men. Indeed, it was bravely drawn from you before. War-death has taken each of them. I have no one left who can hold the sword or polish the plated cup"—so he buries the treasure in a barrow. "Sorrowful he wept," the poet adds, "though night and day, until death's flood touched his heart." That story not only repeats the themes of mortality and the transience of material wealth; to some scholars it suggests that after the loss of his people, his remaining attachment was only to the treasure. They believe he actually *becomes* the dragon, transformed in shape as the love of his heart changed from his fellow human beings to the wealth they'd acquired—an Ebeneezer Scrooge story of the most astonishing sort. We can't tell for certain, because the manuscript is damaged at that point, but that's a stimulating reading because it reinforces themes we see elsewhere in the poem and it fits other stories we know of dragons: an instance of greed and murder created the dragon that Sigemund slew.

The Anglo-Saxons seem to have believed in dragons: one of their maxims, statements about the way the world works, says that a dragon will seek out and sit on a treasure, hoarding it and keeping it from others. Perhaps they believed that dragons were just bad men, all the more dangerous than other people because of their excessive love of wealth and violence in keeping it from others and acquiring more.

For the Anglo-Saxon success wasn't just in acquiring the treasure, but in using it properly to reward, honor, and protect one's people.

Another digression creates a comparison for the sorrow one experiences when a loss or a crime must go unavenged. Beowulf says that the feeling one endures after such an experience is like that of the father who sees his son swinging on the gallows. He can never feel content thereafter: his heart and body grow barren, his home lies deserted, and at night he remains sleepless, thinking his world too big and his life too long.

That story says a lot about how the Anglo-Saxons felt about vengeance, but it also encapsulates the general human experience of loss and grief, another dose of realism in a story some readers want to see as no more than fantasy. Sooner or later, it happens to everyone.

A final digression appears as a messenger returns from the dragon battle to tell the Geats the outcome. He recites not only the event, but past events that will affect the near future of the people. They must remember, he says, how Hygelac attacked the Hugas and Frisians, and how the Swedes killed Haethcyn, Hygelac's older brother, and Hygelac pursued them and avenged his brother—those feuds, suspended during Beowulf's reign, will be renewed when outsiders learn of Beowulf's death, that he no longer lives to protect his folk. The poem hints often at the evils of feuding: typically a feud doesn't end until all of one or both of the feuding parties are dead.

Regardless of the sense of offended honor, someone must know, the poet shows us, when to stop.

The Application

Just as *Beowulf*'s audience would have, we can find practical applications for each of the above digressions.

The models of good and bad kings and queens remind us that we often learn by example. If we tell—and show—the generations that follow us that success means killing, abusing others, stealing and hoarding, and that we can remain successful by lying and cheating, by ignoring responsibilities and thinking only of ourselves, they will learn those lessons and practice them. We're willing to learn the lesson that life is about winning at all costs and that business is about profit at all costs: some say, make your money and move on before someone finds your mistakes.

Beowulf certainly applauds those who boldly seek achievement and success, who know how to use power wisely, and who earn status and reward. But it establishes the difference between those who do so responsibly and generously and those who do so irresponsibly and greedily. Difficulties and defeats may befall even those who behave righteously, but at least such persons won't bring downfall and disgrace upon themselves or others. We have a duty to follow just laws, to consider others' needs, and to reward others' accomplishments as we would our own. That means we do business vigorously and enjoy what we earn, but we realize that *ethics* goes with any sort of business we pursue. "Business ethics" not only isn't an oxymoron, as some wags would have it; it's essentially a redundancy. You may escape the abuses and excesses you commit, but your children, your community, and the reputation you leave behind finally won't.

The Hildeburh and Freawaru stories show us that we shouldn't expect more reward than we ultimately get—even if we deserve it. You're unlikely ever to get paid what you've earned, though it's true that some people at the top of the scale get paid far more than they could ever earn. You're far more likely to have someone thrust you into a position that's good for him or her and not necessarily for you: remain vigilant.

Many of the mistakes we make in relationships—professional or personal—come from our insistence on trying to make people conform to the image we have of them or to the role we want for them, rather than accepting who they are and what they want for themselves. The key here is to try to understand who you are and what you want and resist anyone's desire to enslave you to his or her will. In business that translates into a few principles:

1. Be as careful as you can about the jobs you accept; before you begin learn everything you can about the company and the tasks you must perform.

2. Get the best contract you can and live up to it yourself.

3. Most of us have had to take lesser jobs than we wanted with less pay than we wanted. In such a case, to the greatest degree of your ability, refuse to let your employer abuse you or other employees, and work to put yourself in a position to earn more.

4. Prepare for the worst. Don't assume your company or job will continue indefinitely. Learn, learn, learn, so that you can make a move, either to a different position or a different company, if you wish or if you must.

5. Don't assume you're working for a benevolent management, nor should you assume you're working for a group of beasts. Fulfill your responsibilities, gather information, and reserve your trust.

6. Beware of the insidious egotism that infects some managers and that allows them to believe that other people must or even should do exactly as they say. Leaders must give orders, but they should do so with the good of the organization and the individual employee in mind, not out of a desire to enslave others to their will. Such behavior may briefly intimidate others into compliance, but in the long run it leads to failure, hatred, and a general collapse of authority and productivity.

7. If you're working for a leader you can't trust, look instead for one you can. If you have no choice, remember that your commitment to the leader seldom if ever trumps your commitment to the greater

> principles of the organization or to
> humanity. You should hope that the
> people who work for you think that
> way, too. If they do, perhaps one day
> they'll save you from a terrible blunder.

The "Lay of the Last Survivor" and the story of the lonely father both address loss and how we deal with it. They suggest that even in the worst times we must maintain our courage, our drive, and our humanity—more easily said than done, no doubt. Yet they provide models of lost individuals who succumb to grief. In doing so they encourage us to seek and value affiliations knowing that one day our affiliates will dissolve or die. The alternative, exile or isolationism, is worse, because it is deadly in the present: it allows no future. Being human means confronting sadness, at least at some point. If you've never been sad, you lack compassion; if you're sad too much of the time, you've fallen into either self-pity or sentimentality. *Beowulf* says, even while you seek achievement and affiliation, put yourself in a position to minimize losses or at least the possible catastrophic effects of losses.

Plan, prepare, reinforce, grow within your means, seek trustworthy alliances. Know and practice the difference between profiting and profiteering. If you're a hero, people may fear you; that can produce good or bad results. If you become a dragon, everyone will hate you, and that can't produce good results.

The final digression we considered is about both memory and predicting what will come. The messenger reminds the people of possible enemies ahead. You may think that cruel considering that he has just told them about the death of their king and protector. He would say it's not cruel, but prudent, even necessary. If you remember your past, friends or enemies, you know what alliances you may seek and what dangers you must plan against; if you look ahead to your future, you may realize your preparations and limit if not prevent the affects of oncoming trouble. You may also discern new patterns for success not part of your current plan. Even a disaster may open up avenues for heroic achievement, if one proceeds with attention, compassion, and commitment.

Many people look at their careers much as a writer may look at a plot: a progression of events through a series of important moments toward a goal. Don't be afraid to live in the digressions. They may give you new ideas, find you new friends, teach you new lessons that will help you reach your goals more quickly and completely than if you'd stayed the simple (or simplistic) course.

The Manager's Spotlight

Digressions are really about learning. If you or your employees have a chance to learn something that's in any conceivable way useful to you, them, or the company, as long as it isn't illegal or unethical, let it happen. Too many managers restrict their employees' opportunities or limit their own vision. Organizations stay afloat both by honoring tradition and by preparing for and enacting change. You can't manage successfully without vision. Don't expect your employees to work without a little visionary indulgence of their own.

I'm not encouraging frivolity—entirely. But if you must make a decision about what research or education to permit, err on the permissive side to the degree that you can afford it. Almost any sort of learning helps you and the organization in the long run, even if it means you may lose a better-educated employee to a better job. Better that than keep a frustrated, underemployed worker who will resent you and your company and poison the waters. The best balance may come in discussing your digressions with your own boss and your subordinates' digressions with them to see how you and they together can best reach potentials for mutual success.

Each employee's life or career is just as important to him or her as yours is to you.

Points to Ponder

1. *Think about the best class or other learning experience that you've ever had that didn't obviously impact your job performance: what did it do for you, and why is that important?*

2. *Conversations typically don't keep to one topic, but instead digress at least occasionally even if they do reach a desired conclusion. Think about recent conversations you've had at work or outside work: when you digressed, why did you? when conversation partners digressed, why did they? What did you either learn or accomplish through those digressions?*

3. *Think of the best innovations you've encountered: try to trace how they came about, whether offshoots of old ideas, modifications of pre-existent technologies, variations on old techniques to fit new markets, or by any other means you can establish.*

20

Maxims—and the Big Ideas

Understanding is best—everywhere. . . .

(i.e., Learn. Then learn more.)

The Idea

Almost every culture has its *maxims*: sayings, apothegms, aphorisms, proverbs, neat little locutions that briefly and memorably encapsulate bits of wisdom.

The Anglo-Saxons loved them. The *Beowulf* poet loved them. We love them.

Think of some you know. Perhaps you've even used one today. "A stitch in time saves nine." "Better late than never." "Better to have loved and lost than never to have loved at all." "Name the tune, pay the piper." "The early bird catches the worm." We have thousands of them. Some of them even seem to contradict each other: "look before you leap," but "nothing ventured, nothing gained."

Of course, maxims don't necessarily have in them any inherent truth; their truth derives from context. If we take them as guides for living, their utter simplicity will undermine our ability to deal with complex situations. Some parents will say, when a child asks to borrow some money, "As Shakespeare says, 'Neither a borrower nor a lender be.'" We can find at least two problems there. First, if your child has read *Hamlet*, he or she will know that *Shakespeare* doesn't say that, speaking for himself; his character Polonius says that, and Polonius is a doddering old fool. Second, if your child is old enough to know how you bought your home, he or she will probably then ask why the bank gave you a loan to do it. Upstarts, these kids.

But, right or wrong in any particular instance, maxims have power. Their clarity, brevity, and artful phrasing give us a quick, cutting entryway into problems which we may then accept or reject. Occasionally, as in *Beowulf*, the maxims give us direct insight into a culture by telling us what principles they placed foremost as they prepared to act.

In this chapter we'll look at several of the maxims or aphorisms in *Beowulf* and try to determine if they tell us anything we can use on the job. Some of them contradict assumptions of our own time or even dicta from our modern religions; nonetheless, they tell us something quite *human*: they ring with an authority that arrests our attention even if we choose to reject them as guides for action.

And most beowulfian maxims deal with action: urging us to take it rather than remain passive and let the world act upon us. At least then we have some say in what happens to us.

Of course, when we put them together the maxims in *Beowulf* contribute to what your English teacher would call *themes*: the major idea or ideas an author aims to communicate through his or her work. Any particular work may have one or several themes or even no special theme at all: potboilers written purely for entertainment, especially those of more recent times, often don't express, explore, or promote a theme, but works of earlier literature almost always do. They may communicate messages about religion, social behavior, politics, personal virtue, or any other area of thought through which we examine and try to improve the human condition. For our purposes we may just call them:

"The Big Ideas."

We're not talking here about what Edward G. Robinson in 1930s gangster movies and Bugs Bunny in old cartoons mean when they say, "What's da big idea?" Usually they mean, "why are you standing in my way?" or "why are you bothering me?" We're talking about what the poet meant *Beowulf* to be *about*, truths for the audience to carry with them into day-to-day living long after they'd ceased to think about the excitement and fun of the poem's adventures. So let's list the big ideas.

First, since life is always tough and danger or trouble may sit waiting around any bend in the road, we need to *maintain steadfast courage*. Even with courage we may fail, the poet says, but without it we're lost. We must expect to meet challenges and do so when they come, not only when we believe we'll be most ready for them.

Second, therefore, we must *vigilantly prepare* for future difficulties by seeking training, experience, knowledge, and wisdom that will help us survive them and succeed.

Third, while we do well to pursue our talents and skills to gain success, we do best when, in addition to achieving our own goals, we also *treat others with generosity and honor*. Doing so wins allies; failing to do so makes enemies of would-be friends.

Fourth, we must *avoid arrogance*, which leads to complacency and foolish decisions.

Fifth and sixth, mortality dooms us all at last; our best stays against mortality are to *fulfill our responsibilities* and *live a life worth living*. By making the most of our abilities and developing and enjoying them in the present, we limit the otherwise paralyzing effects of the fear of mortality and leave something behind that can make life better for those who follow us.

Seventh, we owe a debt of loyalty to those persons who have put us in positions to succeed and enjoy our lives. We repay that debt by *remembering and appreciating our predecessors* and *earning the loyalty of those who follow us* through achievement and laudable actions.

That's a substantial and impressive list of big ideas for one little book, and that's one of the reasons why I told you in the introduction that *Beowulf* is a marvelous, if not miraculous, book.

The Passage

Again we have *passages*, several rather than one. We'll look at each maxim and what it means, then in the next section we'll try to determine what we can use from them all.

1. "Just so must a young man bring about good through gifts of treasure to his father's followers, so that afterwards he may dwell with willing comrades and save the people when war comes." That one comes early in the poem. It specifies that children must learn generosity from their parents and practice it if they want desirable results in the long run.

2. "Woe be to those who through dire deeds thrust the spirit into the fire's embrace: they may expect no comfort."

That line holds not only a Christian message, but a general warning against either false religion or seeking violence for its own sake.

3. "Each of these things must a keen soldier strive to know: words and deeds." The Danish coast guard warns Beowulf that speaking fine words is impressive, but performing the great deed is an entirely different matter.

4. Fate often preserves the undoomed man, if his courage holds." Beowulf says that when he describes his great youthful contest against Breca, when both sought to prove their strength and courage. He says, ironically, that fate may preserve you and it may not, if you remain courageous. If you don't, you haven't a chance—that means no one can undertake a grand task with a great likelihood of success.

5. "Understanding is best everywhere. . . . He who long enjoys the world in these days of strife must experience much of both loved ones and enemies." Good and bad come alike to anyone who lives long enough, so the most useful quality for one to develop is the ability to understand how the world works and treat people justly.

6. "Enjoy while you can the meed of the many, and leave to your kin a people and a kingdom when you must depart to meet your creator." Wealhtheow, the Danish queen, tells Beowulf—and reminds her husband—that we do best to enjoy our accomplishments while we

can and arrange so that when we die, our children will inherit enough from us so that they may live well, too.

7. "It is better for everyone that he avenge his friend than that he mourn too much." After Grendel's Mother kills Hrothgar's friend and counselor to avenge the death of her son, Beowulf reminds the king that he, too, has the duty to avenge his loss. While according to Christian thought people should leave vengeance to God rather than taking it themselves, for the ancient Germanic peoples vengeance was part of their legal and cultural fabric.

8. "He trusted in the strength of his mighty hand-grip; so must a man do when in battle he expects to win lasting fame: he dwells not at all on life." The main point here isn't about Beowulf's hand-grip, but about battle: once he gets in it, he trusts his ability and fights without fretting about death, which would distract him and perhaps cause him to lose.

9. "It is wonderful to say how mighty God with spacious spirit gives wisdom, land, and nobility to the human race—he wields power over all." While the poem has few if any explicitly Christian references (though some clear allusions to the Jewish Bible), it expresses a fair number of religious sentiments. Here Hrothgar points out that we should feel thankful for what we get and appreciate that God has power over the world—we don't.

10. "Treasure can easily overcome anyone of the human race: heed this he who will." The poet reminds the reader of the tug of greed that draws us every chance it gets.

11. "The judgment of God would govern the deeds of every man, as it does even now." The poet reminds us to practice kindness and justice in the world, since in the end God governs us justly.

12. "Kinship can never be put aside by anyone who thinks rightly." Family and heritage determine, inescapably, a great deal of who we are.

13. "Death is better for each man than a life of reproach." Wiglaf chastises those of Beowulf's soldiers who fled the dragon when their lord needed them.

14. "It is a wonder when a brave man reaches the end of his allotted life." We never quite believe that the great persons will die. They probably don't believe it either. We come to see the great as too good to die. Sadly, we still wish for immortality in this world.

15. "It is fitting that one praise his lord and friend when he's led forth from his body." Nearly all cultures have some sort of funeral customs that laud those who have lived well. They have earned it, and we benefit from praising them.

16. "Fate always goes as it must." While this maxim appears early in the poem, before Beowulf meets Grendel, I place it last because it summarizes the wisdom that the poem aims to teach. The first

word in the line, *wyrd* in Old English, has no exact translation in modern English. Most scholars use *fate* as I have. The word is the ancestor of our modern word *weird*, and Shakespeare uses it in Macbeth to describe the witches who delude Macbeth, the "Weird Sisters." It actually means something like "the way things happen." The last word in the line is *sceal*, ancestor of our modern word *shall*, but it has a little stronger connotation than that, something closer to *must*. So the line means most accurately something like: "Things work out however they're going to." You may look at that and say "duh," but it's something that at one time or another most of us have heard from our grandparents, when they try to keep us from worrying too much about how events will turn out, especially those beyond our control.

The Application

Let's trace application for each of the maxims.

1. Learn generosity from your elders, practice it yourself, and teach it to your children. In the long run, even if it doesn't bring you returns, it may save those who come after you. Companies do well to remember that maximum profit in the short run doesn't always mean maximum profit—or even survival—in the long run.

2. Most religions teach us that evil catches
    up to us, visiting not only us but our
    children.   Avoiding it may not be
    enough to help one prosper, but submit-
    ting to it initiates disaster.

3. Boasting, making jokes at others'
    expense, and making promises may get
    you elected to public office or win
    laughter from your friends, but in
    the long run you'll have to back up
    words with deeds. Speak less than you
    would and do more than you promised:
    that brings less trouble and greater
    profit in the long run—and the *Beowulf*
    poet is thoroughly concerned, and
    hopes we are, with what happens in the
    long run.

4. Beowulf teaches confidence and action:
    you may not succeed with them, but
    you can't succeed without them.   So
    press on and defy your enemies.

5. Everyone experiences good and ill—
    both in events and in the people we
    meet—so we do best to try to learn how
    the world works and how to use that
    knowledge, but also show understand-
    ing and compassion toward those who
    fail.

6. It's good to enjoy life, praise and fame,
    but remember that they pass quickly
    enough—and so will you.   So do the
    best you can to provide for those who
    survive you.   The Anglo-Saxons had
    no notion of insurance or trust funds,
    but had they, they would have encour-
    aged us to use them justly and gener-
    ously.

7. I think the best way to use this maximum is to look at it as an encouragement to action: when things go wrong, it's better to *do* something than to mope and worry.

8. You can't succeed in the arena if your mind dwells on the possibility of failure. You must live in the moment, give your full effort, believe you can succeed, and clear your mind for victory.

9. Remember that you can make choices about your own actions, but you're not in control of the whole world, nor are you responsible for everything— only for your choices. Faith builds confidence, and confidence builds strength.

10. Ah, once again the problem of greed: earning is good, for the security it can give you and your family; clinging to wealth or obsessing over it leads to catastrophe, because you forget the persons for whose good you earned it.

11. The point here is to avoid limiting yourself to short-term thinking. Many people act in the present as though there were no future. Whether or not you win fame and glory in the present, the poet asks, how will history judge you? How will God judge you? Have you acted selfishly or considerately? Too many people allow themselves the simple lie that "it's all about me."

12. We'll discuss later the great importance of family to the poem, but here we must recognize that who you are and where

you come from does make a difference in what you do and how you live. For good or ill others will judge you by your family, and you will always have a responsibility to them and through them a connection to your roots. Your genetic material as well as your background, social and geographical, affect what opportunities are likely to arise for you and what constitutional strengths you have to exploit them.

13. The worst thing about a bad action isn't what others think of you—though that's bad enough—it's what you think of yourself. If you think of yourself as a thief or a fool or a coward, you're more likely to act like one. If you're convinced you can't accomplish a task, you can't. However: that isn't an endorsement to try something foolhardy that's dangerously beyond your ability. With confidence must go prudence.

14. Sadness and death are inescapable parts of life. Many people refuse to confront mortality until they must. A good death, though, one that leaves people with hope and admiration for the deceased, has a glory of its own. We may apply the same point to retirement: some look forward to it, others dread it, because it takes them from the arena they love. It must come; one must prepare.

15. We should praise and remember those who have served as models of success and goodness. Through them we praise what's best in human nature and encourage ourselves to fulfill our best

potentials.   Praise encourages due appreciation and hope.

16. Sometimes bad things do happen to good people—they also happen to bad people. Remember the old saw about changing for the better what you can, but knowing the difference between what you can change and what you can't. Carry your weight, not the weight of the world.

These maxims add up to a way of looking at life and the world. It's a better world if we believe wisdom is at least possible, and possibly attainable. Notions of wisdom sometimes change from one culture to another or from one age to another, but some remain pretty consistent over time. You may do well by acquiring knowledge; you can only be great by seeking wisdom. The ancients believed in wisdom; I don't know if we do anymore. At the end of Alexandre Dumas's famous novel *The Count of Monte Cristo*, the hero comes to this discovery: all human wisdom is contained in two words, *wait* and *hope*. I once shared that line with a friend. She answered that Dumas hadn't got it quite right: he should have said *pray* and *hope*. The Beowulf poet would I think have said, *act* and *believe*.

The Manager's Spotlight

Today we often feel afraid to share gems of wisdom from the past because they sound corny or trite. In one sense, we should distrust maxims—they're often too brief to be clear, too general to be helpful, and too apt to contradict one another.

But sometimes a saying will exactly encapsulate an idea or experience so that it will spur people to action. Don't be afraid to share the gems you find with your colleagues. Share *them. Unless you're a preacher, avoid preaching them. A great maxim can become a shared call to action that helps give a group cohesiveness and focus.*

Avoid, however, letting it become a limitation. Words should serve us, not enslave us. Try the maxim, and if it helps, use it.

Points to Ponder

1. *What's the difference between a maxim and a* slogan? *What purpose does either serve?*

2. *Collect a list of five or ten aphorisms. What do you find in them that's true? What do you find that's simplistic and limiting (or even false)?*

3. *Take your favorite maxim from this chapter; how can you apply it to a situation you're experiencing in your own life?*

21

The Value of Speeches

Not at all was he silent, the messenger,
but spoke truly to all.

(i.e., Training gets you a job; speaking and writing well build you a career.)

The Idea

A good public speech can strongly motivate an audience, while a poor one produces all sorts of deleterious effects, anything from arousing scorn to inhibiting positive action to inspiring a backlash of negative action. In this chapter we'll examine some of the important speeches in *Beowulf* to determine what speakers say, why they say it, and how they say it to achieve such ends as a good speech can accomplish. While this chapter is, like the last one, rather longer than most of the others, it enumerates strategies that can help you enormously in career building.

Take your time with it, and use what helps most. You may even want to break it up into two or three reading sessions, noting the most important points you get from each.

The poet when about to record a speech normally first identifies the speaker and then uses the word *mathelode*. We translate that word as *spoke*, as in "Hrothgar spoke" or "Beowulf spoke," but we may better translate it as "made a formal speech"—a cumbersome expression, but more accurate. Important characters in the world of the poem find themselves in situations that call for formal speaking. To speak well shows wisdom and good leadership. To do poorly undermines others' confidence and limits one's opportunities to accomplish anything worthwhile.

That's true for us as well. The ability to speak well (and write well) can turn a job into a career. Poor speeches tend to diminish an audience's respect for a speaker, even if the speaker has achieved other successes. Not every good writer turns out to be a good speaker; in fact, many aren't, so even they must practice speaking. If you have a knack for public speaking, you can still improve by writing better and by honing your delivery. If you have no affinity for it, you can still do passably well with study, practice, and some boosts to your confidence.

You can find many resources, everything from college courses to public lectures to dozens of self-help books aimed to help you become a better speaker. Many people have difficulty with public speaking not because they lack intelligence or verbal skill, but because they freeze: the presence of an audience in a formal setting terrifies them. Courses and good books can help you acquire strategies, but only practice in public situations can give the assurance that you can succeed as a speaker.

If you're one of those persons who simply can't master public speaking, take heart: most of us *don't have to do it*. You can live a perfectly happy and successful life without achieving praise and fame for speeches. However, if you can acquire the rudimentary knowledge and skills and move toward success as a speaker, you'll open up many new roads that will otherwise

remain closed to you. If you find you can't get yourself to follow those roads, by studying speeches you can at least learn
what others do so that you can understand how they succeed,
or you can see how they fail so that you can refuse to allow
them to mystify and mislead you—perhaps equally important
skills.

The poet who composed *Beowulf* didn't construct a how-to
manual on public speaking, but we can tease out some points
of interest by examining the important speeches that appear in
the poem. They show us what speakers in those days found
important and effective. So let's evaluate the techniques to
determine whether or not we can profitably adopt them.

You'll find that a few consistent principles guide the construc-
tion of speeches in the poem. Those principles fit the instructive purpose of the book, clarifying the themes we considered
in the previous chapter.

The good speaker is honest and confident, has a clear point in
mind, and encourages the listeners to practice good behavior—
no one speaks just to speak, to call attention to himself without
offering some service or information. The speaker appeals to
tradition and provides evidence or well-known stories to support the point of the speech. Speakers are not shy about sup-
plying their credentials, or even bragging a bit, to give the
speech legitimacy, nor do they hesitate to refute opponents—
though normally they give them opportunity to save face.
They don't fear a degree of formality or even grandness in their
delivery: they want to seem authoritative and to make the
moment memorable.

That's a pretty good set of instructions: a bit different than, but
sharing much in common with, what you'll hear from speech
gurus today. We do get the sense that speakers still follow for-
mulas, so we, like the Anglo-Saxons, and like the Greeks and

Romans before them, must believe that a person can learn to speak well.

Now let's look at a few examples. We'll skip the speeches in the insult match between Beowulf and Breca and those that aim mostly to convey information and focus instead on those that have "rhetorical" purpose, that is, speeches that establish or argue a point so as to change audience behavior.

The Passage

The first two formal speeches in the poem occur when Beowulf and his men arrive on the shore of Denmark, hoping to get Hrothgar's permission to fight Grendel. First the coast guard spots the Geats and formally asks their mission, then Beowulf formally replies.

The coast guard asks who the travelers are, notes that he has seen them come by sea and that his task is to watch the shore. He observes that they come openly, not stealthily, and adds that they are not certain of receiving welcome and must know that themselves. He compliments Beowulf's demeanor and bearing: "Never have I seen a greater man among the nobles of the earth—may his appearance never belie him!" He asks their lineage, so that he may know they're not spies, then concludes with a maxim aimed to hasten their reply and so either diffuse any tension he or they may be experiencing from the encounter or give him the warning he needs to race to the court with news of invasion. "Quickest is best to make known whence you've come," he says.

Each part of that speech has a specific function and no wasted words. The speaker means business, asks immediately for the information he needs without being impolite. In fact, he compliments the apparent leader of the troop, probably to show that, without abasing himself, he is simply doing his job, not intending to insult persons who have arrived on a legitimate mission. Asking their lineage will tell him more than asking their names or country of origin: if they come on an errand from an important family, he will have heard of them—the world was smaller in those days—and will know something of their history and disposition. The speech accomplishes his goal perfectly.

Beowulf is a fairly young man when he undertakes the Grendel adventure, but his reply shows the poise, maturity, and confidence that he must display to gain permission to speak with the king. The poet says that the hero "unlocked his word-hoard"; that implies not that he pulled out a dictionary to impress the coast guard with big words, but that he understood he needed to shape a typical sort of formal answer to the Dane's questions.

He names their tribe and their king, adding that they are Hygelac's "hearth-companions," that is, family, close friends, or most trusted soldiers of a well-known king. Beowulf tells his father's name and notes his reputation, but doesn't give his own name: the Dane didn't ask that. He adds immediately that they seek Hrothgar with a friendly heart, and he asks the man for counsel about the problems the Danes have had with Grendel, so that he might know best how to approach Hrothgar. Then he adds, confidently, "I can teach Hrothgar, that wise and good man, a plan for how he can vanquish the fiend."

To the coast guard's formal address, Beowulf gives a specific point-by-point answer. He embellishes the final point a bit, but otherwise he returns a polite, direct, informative answer, tuned with a bit of *savoir faire*, to a polite, urgent, no-nonsense question.

Beowulf delivers another formal speech when he gains audience with Hrothgar. He begins by wishing Hrothgar good health, names his king, mentions with some details the heroic deeds of his youth, explains how he has heard of Grendel, and expresses his reason for coming to Denmark: he requests a boon, that he, alone, may fight the monster. He adds that he intends to fight "fairly," without weapons, since Grendel uses none, and so that his king may be particularly proud of him. He even uses a bit of grim humor: Grendel will be as eager to eat Geats as Danes, and if he defeats Beowulf, they won't have to worry about disposing of the hero's body. He concludes with the famous maxim, "Fate always goes as it must."

Now that is a fairly long speech for someone who has just come before the king, but Beowulf must impress Hrothgar with absolute commitment and fortitude if he's going to get the job he wants. The speech rather eloquently follows the pattern that many of us use in job application letters: complimentary greeting, pedigree, brief rehearsal of experience, clear request, and something memorable and compelling to bring the reader's memory back to the letter—though humor works better in speeches than in letters. Some writers or speakers prefer to follow a pleasant greeting immediately with their statement of purpose, but Beowulf chooses to precede the request with a statement of his people's endorsement of his heroism, so that when he makes the request, it doesn't seem entirely out of line. Some readers may find that information dangerously close to bragging, but in its time it would have sounded little different to the audience than it would now if one were to say, "I've just graduated with highest honors in electrical engineering from MIT."

Hrothgar then gives formal reply to Beowulf's formal request—a pattern that we see often in the poem, where one formal gesture precipitates or requires another. The king refers to Beowulf as "my friend," a neutral but at least not negative beginning (Beowulf diffuses his insult match with Hunferth by calling him "my friend"). Hrothgar recalls how in his younger years he took in Beowulf's father and settled a feud for him. Then he rehearses some of his own family history and bemoans the current state of terror caused by Grendel. Hrothgar says that, if He wished, God could set things right, then he invites Beowulf to join them for feasting and revelry— without answering the young man's question. Only after the feast, when the king has observed him a bit, and after Beowulf has passed his test with Hunferth, does Hrothgar grant the hero his request, turning over the defense of the hall to him for the night.

That speech has several interesting points. Hrothgar admits his need, but doesn't yet accept Beowulf's suit. He hints that the result is in God's hands rather than in any man's. He admits Beowulf into the court, but suspends his decision. The speech is honest, but prudent: Hrothgar isn't in a position to brag about how his own soldiers have dealt with Grendel. It does recognize Beowulf's debt to Hrothgar, but the king doesn't want to place either the court or the young hero in greater danger than they already face until he has a better sense of the young man who dares make such a bold request. The king arouses sympathy. He avoids insulting a possible benefactor or over-encouraging a young man who to his knowledge is not yet fully proven. A calming speech follows a bold one that could have produced an outpouring of various powerful emotions: overeagerness from his guest, resentment from his own soldiers, imprudent decisions. Deft.

The next important speech is delivered by Wealhtheow, the Danish queen, in two parts as the court celebrates Beowulf's victory over Grendel. She passes among the soldiers, serving drink—a task allotted to the queen to show her lord's generosity and her closeness to her people, not demeaning in the eyes of the ancient Germanic peoples. First, she speaks to Hrothgar as she fills his cup, asking that he generously reward the Geats for Beowulf's heroism. Second, she mentions that she heard that Hrothgar had said he wished Beowulf were his own son, and she cautions him that he should leave his kingdom to his blood kin. She also indirectly addresses their nephew Hrothulf, who will succeed to the kingship if Hrothgar dies before one of his sons is old enough to rule. Third, she says she's sure he will rule justly and with kindness toward her sons if he becomes king. What the poem doesn't tell but that the audience knew is that historically when Hrothgar died, Hrothulf tried by violence to take the throne from his cousin who by then should have succeeded, and he burnt Heorot to the ground in the attempt. So we get from the first part of the speech that Wealhtheow is trying to take care of her sons and that she guesses they will have trouble before they can grow up to defend themselves.

During the second part of her speech she gives Beowulf a famous heirloom necklace, probably the greatest treasure she has to offer, and says that she hopes he will prosper, grow in skill, be happy, and protect her sons should they need it. Then, probably speaking to the whole court, she proclaims that everyone there is honorable and loyal. Again, she tries to encourage both the visiting hero and the local soldiers to remain true to the king. She acts generously, and her speech is gentle and subtle, but she makes her wishes clearly known. She hasn't the king's power to command, but she has the opportunity and ability to affect how people think and what they do: essentially, she warns everyone about Hrothulf without insulting him, asks Beowulf's assistance, and rewards the hero ahead of time for what she hopes he will do.

Beowulf won't be on hand to prevent Hrothulf's violence, but before he goes home, he offers to train the princes at Hygelac's court. Since he's from another country and has his own duties, that's probably the best he can do, so Wealhtheow's speech

works on him if not on her own people. The speeches all succeed, at least in the short run.

Several speeches occur after Grendel's Mother takes vengeance
for her son. The best one for our purposes occurs right before
Beowulf enters the lake to fight the she-beast. Addressing
Hrothgar as "renowned one" and "wise king" and citing the
king's lineage, he claims he is eager for this next adventure. He
asks that, if he should die in the battle, Hrothgar might act
as a father to the comrades he leaves behind and send the treasures he has won to Hygelac. He compliments Hrothgar's generosity by saying he enjoyed those treasures while he could.
Then he asks that Hrothgar give Hunferth, who has lent
Beowulf a special sword for this battle, his own heirloom
sword as a replacement. That brief speech honors his host,
declares his intention, disposes of his belongings, takes care of
his colleagues, and diffuses any lingering resentment that
Hunferth may have had, eliminating the possibility of
vengeance for previous words—a lot to accomplish in a few
brief lines.

Good models: speakers aim for clarity, brevity, pith.

When Beowulf returns from the lake with Grendel's head and
the hilt of the sword with which he has killed Grendel's
Mother, Hrothgar makes one of the most famous speeches in
the poem. Some scholars call it "Hrothgar's Sermon," because
it exhorts Beowulf particularly but the audience in general to
generosity and good behavior. He assures Beowulf of exactly
what he came to get: praise and fame, but then exhorts him to
guard them patiently and to balance strength with prudence.
You'll be a comfort to your people, Hrothgar says, as Heremod
was not—the evil king guilty of murder and hoarding. Instruct
yourself by his bad example, Hrothgar tells Beowulf, and so
understand the truth about mature virtue. "It's wonderful to
say," he adds, "how mighty God gives earthly gifts and wis-

dom, kingdoms and glories to some, but often they grow prideful and don't realize that evil lies ahead. Then when it comes, the time in which they prospered seems all too short and their riches all too little, and avarice consumes them. Guard against such ills, and remember that your strength lasts only for a time: death comes to all. Look what happened to me through the depredations of Grendel. Thank god I have lived to see the end of that suffering. Now we shall feast, and in the morning I will share with you a great many treasures." Appreciation, good advice humbly delivered, and controlled emotion mark that speech.

When Beowulf departs, he tells Hrothgar—and, indirectly, Wealhtheow, that he will always do for them and their sons whatever he can. Hrothgar compliments him: "The knowing Lord put that in your mind: I have never heard such a young man speak so wisely. You are not only strong, but also clear in mind and sound of speech. Should Hygelac's family fade, the Geats could do no better than choose you their king. You have brought enduring friendship between our peoples."

The first speech may in its seriousness have the effect of dampening the joy of Beowulf's victories, so we may assume that Hrothgar observed in Beowulf something that led him to warn the young man about pride and about enjoying treasures too much. Another way to read it, though, is that Hrothgar, recognizing his own weakness, suffers an outpouring of his fears. We know that sometimes people speak not to their audiences as much as to themselves. In the morning he doesn't recant the warning, but hearing Beowulf's peaceful and generous intentions, he amends what he said the night before by declaring Beowulf fit to rule, not likely to give in to lust for power and excessive wealth.

No matter how good we are, everyone can use the occasional warning or reminder, and no matter how great one's humility, everyone benefits from honest and loving praise. Hrothgar's speeches together accomplish both ends.

The final speeches we'll consider in this chapter, two by Beowulf and two by Wiglaf, appear in association with the dragon battle. They express ideas and sentiments appropriate to the preparation for battle, engagement in battle, and the aftermath of battle—but we may think of them as preparation for action and assessment of action.

First, Beowulf, in the longest speech in the poem (besides perhaps his recounting his Danish adventure), prepares himself and his people for his death. "In youth I survived many battles. I was but seven winters old when King Hrethel took me from my father to raise me. Nor was I less to him than his own sons, the eldest of whom, sadly, by accident, struck down his brother with a stray arrow. It's like that when a father must watch his son swing from the gallows, a sorrow without recompense. He lingers on, waiting for death, as did the Geats' king. Then came strife between Geats and Swedes. The second son, Haethcyn, was slain, but lord Hygelac avenged that. I, too, repaid Hrethel's generosity in that battle, and for that Hygelac granted me land and a home here, nor had he need to seek a better warrior from other lands. I always walked the point, and so will always do, while my strength lasts. Now as guardian of the people I'll seek one more glorious deed in this feud against the dragon. I'd go without sword and weapon as I did against Grendel, if I knew how to grapple against the fire and poison of the beast. But I tell you this, I will not flee one foot from the monster. I'm still hardy of heart and will refrain from boasting, but now between the two of us victory must go as fate bestows it. This is not your task, but mine alone. With courage I must gain his gold, or battle will take me."

That speech may seem to serve little rhetorical purpose, but it actually accomplishes several important ends. It states Beowulf's intentions, let's his followers who won't be able to stand against the dragon off the hook, settles his own mind that even a victory will mean his own death, and reminds his people that they will likely face renewed feuds from old enmities once he's gone. It's a thoroughly pragmatic speech, fueled by responsibility, but also spilling over with Beowulf's defining trait, the one that both makes him and breaks him, heroism. It is perhaps a bit self-centered, but imagine how you would feel if you were about to go out and get yourself burnt to cinders: I suspect you'd forgive yourself for a bit of nostalgia.

Next, when Beowulf has engaged battle with the dragon and finds himself engulfed in the monster's fire, Wiglaf, his kinsman and best young soldier, must try to "fire up" the troops to support their king. He directs his speech to their responsibility as Beowulf's *thanes*, or sworn followers. "I remember that time when we drank mead together and promised allegiance to our treasure-giver, that we would repay his generosity in such time as he needed from us sword and courage," Wiglaf says. "He deemed us worthy for this venture, gave us such gear as we use now because he accounted us bold soldiers, though the Lord chose him alone for this glorious, impetuous deed. Now the day has come when our liege-lord needs us: let's step forward to help him while we may! God knows it's better that the fire embrace my body than that I fail. His great deeds merit that he shouldn't suffer alone."

Then Wiglaf joins Beowulf in the dragon fight, and exhorts him to continue: "Great Beowulf, fulfill well the pledge you made in youth, that while you live you'll never let your glory diminish. Now, resolute prince, with famous deeds and all your strength you must defend your life. I will help you!"

The second part of the speech is shorter, because Wiglaf delivers it beneath the dragon's fire, but both aim at the same end, to encourage others to such great deeds as they will need to survive an intractable enemy. Both parts note the *responsibility* and *reputation* of the audience and the *promises* they made and should fulfill. Those are "halftime speeches" of the most serious sort, because life and death, glory and shame hang in the balance. In each part, too, Wiglaf doesn't merely encourage others to act; he speaks and then acts accordingly himself.

Beowulf's final speech follows the death of the dragon. It also falls into two parts, the first before he asks Wiglaf to bring some of the treasure for him to see, the second after he has seen it and as he prepares to die. First he says, "Now I would wish to give war-garments to my son, had I an heir to follow me. For fifty winters I ruled the people, and no king of the surrounding nations dared threaten us. I awaited my fated time, ruled my country, sought no trouble, swore no false oaths. Weak now with deadly wounds, I can have joy in that, so that the Ruler need not reproach me with kin-murder. Now go quickly, beloved Wiglaf, to examine the hoard, that I may see the ancient treasure, the sparkling gems, so that I can the more easily give up the life and country I held so long."

When Wiglaf returns, Beowulf utters his final words. "For these treasures I thank the King of Glory that I was able to win them for my people on my death-day. For them I sold the old portion of my life. Command the soldiers to raise a mound for me on the headland, so that afterwards seafarers will call it 'Beowulf's Barrow.'" He takes from his neck a torque, or neck-ring, the sign of his kingship, and passes it to Wiglaf with these final words: "You're the last of our race. Fate has drawn away all my valorous kinsmen, according to the Great Measurer's decree. I must follow them."

This speech is no rhetorical wonder, but it does serve some important ends. First, he assigns the kingship to Wiglaf, and so appoints a successor. Second, he has the chance to survey his life, and he decides that at least he did no harm, and at best he defended his people from invasion. He doesn't dwell on his victories, but does resolve himself calmly to the death he must confront, partly in the pleasure that with his death he has won treasures for his folk. Most important is what he doesn't say: he does not condemn those soldiers who failed him at need, those who couldn't bring themselves to brave the dragon's fire, nor does he blame them in any way. In fact, he actually refers to them as "battle-friends" and "battle-famed ones," treating kindly a failure that few people would elude.

Notice, too, that the soldiers are thoroughly willing to express their love for each other. Other characters address the hero as "Beloved Beowulf," and he feels comfortable using that epithet in return. We feel shy of such terms today, fearing their sexual implications, but in *Beowulf*'s time such suggestions simply aren't there. Speakers can express love for friends, family, and benefactors without reserve—what a boon that would be to our time!

Perhaps most important, Beowulf, knowing the gravity of the situation, fulfills a king's duty and leaves behind words of wisdom for his people: the moment would lack completeness without such a speech. Sometimes, if your responsibilities are great enough, you just can't get out of it.

Wiglaf, though, does place blame on the soldiers who fled, as we find in his speech that follows. "Lo, he tells the truth who says that your liege-lord, who gave you treasures and war-gear, wasted them when battle arose. He had no reason to boast of his war-companions. But God allowed him that, when he needed courage, he avenged himself. Little protection could I give him: too few defenders thronged to their king

at his need. Now treasure-giving and love of our home-
land must end. Death is better for anyone than a life of
reproach."

As they prepare the funeral pyre, Wiglaf addresses the people:
"Often shall many a man endure exile because of the will of one
man, and so it has come to pass for us. We couldn't persuade
the beloved king not to attack the dragon. He held to his noble
destiny, and destiny was too strong. I brought treasures to
show him while yet he lived, and he spoke many words, commanded me to greet you, asked that you build a pyre and barrow. He was the world's worthiest soldier. I will lead you into
the hoard, and let the pyre be made ready. When we come out,
carry our lord there, where he must long dwell in the Ruler's
protection." Then once they have lit the funeral pyre, he adds,
"Now must the fire consume the prince of warriors, who often
endured showers of iron when a storm of arrows rushed over
the shield wall. The shaft held to its duty, following the arrow-
tip." With the ashes they inter the treasure in Beowulf's burial
mound.

We find in Wiglaf's speech what was absent in Beowulf's: the
young man spares no one his grief and ire at the loss of his
lord. He blames those who fled, and he blames Beowulf himself for fighting the dragon, and he bemoans the trouble ahead
for them all. Aside from Hunferth's failed attempt to defeat
Beowulf in the insult match, Wiglaf's final speeches are probably the most unsuccessful in the poem. Their criticism isn't
constructive, and it accomplishes nothing. And yet who can
blame him? Grief has overtaken him, and he knows his people
have hard times ahead. Sometimes leaders must berate their
charges to gird them for the labors ahead.

And yet I wonder if he couldn't have learned something from
his king: better to forgive and prepare those who have failed
than to strip them of all vestiges of hope: the hopeless certain-

ly will fail. Wiglaf is not the leader Beowulf was, and he knows it; hearing his speech, the people will know that as well. That's probably what the poet hoped through the character of Wiglaf to teach us. The young man is a brave warrior, loyal to his king beyond anything a leader could hope for, but he isn't yet prepared to lead others, and in his grief he is even ungenerous to the king who sacrificed his life for his people. Wiglaf asserts that Beowulf could have avoided the dragon, but by law he had to avenge the attack the dragon had made, and he could hardly believe his people safe with a fire-breather awake, angry, and on the loose.

Good leadership requires not only deeds, but also good words, not only true words, but apt words. From Wiglaf the people don't hear anything to inspire them to meet the trouble ahead—unless criticism will do that—and the poet hints as the poem ends that the Geats will not have sufficient strength or will to repel foreign invaders. Could a speech of encouragement and preparation have avoided that end? Probably not. We could hardly expect another such warrior to appear, but had someone with Beowulf's skill in speaking have emerged, perhaps the Geats could have defended themselves with vigor, buoyed by the hope of success.

Words often set the tone for deeds.

The Application

Let's see if we can't condense from those examples of orations in *Beowulf* some Anglo-Saxon maxims for creating successful, artful speeches that you too may use to advantage.

> 1. Know your audience and their expectations. You are, after all, speaking to them and not to yourself. You may not always want to meet every expectation,

but you should at least know as much about them as you can so you can plan your speech accordingly. Make the audience aware of any connections you have to them.

2. Identify yourself and your background and credentials as you begin. An audience who knows something about you may be more open to what you have to say. Don't, however, overstate your abilities: remain prudent.

3. Know what point you want to make, get to it as briskly as you can, and make it clearly. Clarify your purpose and don't be afraid to say or ask for what you want. Try to find out ahead of time if you're speaking in a delicate situation where tact rather than clarity must rule the day; otherwise, get to the point.

4. Speak confidently and forthrightly. Tell the truth, but stop short of insulting your audience to the point that you lose any further hope of communicating with them—unless you know you'll never again wish to communicate with them, which is seldom likely.

5. Treat your audience politely and compliment them if you can—without becoming sycophantish. Show your appreciation for their positions and accomplishments without belittling your own.

6. Design your speech with a beginning, middle, and end. Use a complimentary opening, include such information as

will help you carry your point, and end with something memorable. If you wish to lengthen a speech, do so by adding data or examples that support your ideas, but make sure that they're on point. A little drama helps, but don't overdo it.

7. A calming speech can have just as much power and just as important an influence as a rousing one.

8. Use a little humor if your subject and situation allow for it, but avoid it if it can undermine the seriousness of the occasion. Today we tend to attempt rather more humor than did the Anglo-Saxons, so this maxim may apply less to us than to them. Then again, it may not. If you've heard a speech in which someone tried to use humor and failed or dwindled into one witticism after another without ever getting to a point, you know the danger of overindulging. Remember it.

9. Show appreciation for your audience's customs, history, and religious faith— and for your own.

10. Most speech coaches encourage us to avoid preachiness. The Anglo-Saxons apparently didn't mind preaching, either doing it or hearing it. The key to success seems to be preaching to yourself as well as to your audience: showing that you don't consider yourself above them, but that what you say applies to you as well as to them or to anyone. And if you preach, let kindness rather than oppression be your guide.

The ancient art of rhetoric aims to encourage people to honorable, generous, laudable action. If you can, avoid reproaching your audience. If you must provide just criticism, offer concrete suggestions for improvement. Don't be afraid to add an apt metaphor, but avoid getting too flowery.

11. If in a speech you dare to make a boast or promise, you'd better have already made an absolute commitment to live up to it.

12. Know the difference between sentiment and sentimentality. Expression of honest feeling can move an audience; lingering on unearned emotion will turn them away in embarrassment.

Most speech coaches from most periods of history would support those maxims: dependable speech techniques tend to persist through time. As with most advice, one does best to sift, keep what's useful, and if not discard the rest, file it for later consideration.

The Manager's Spotlight

You'll probably be called on to make professional speeches periodically. Whether or not you have a natural talent for and find pleasure in public speaking, you can treat each speech as a chance to enhance your public persona, but also to be kind to your audience. If you're terrified of public speaking, buck up and get some professional instruction. If you're loquacious, don't waste people's valuable living time by droning on just to please yourself or your sense of humor. As the Danish coast guard says, normally "briefest is best." Unless someone's paying you to speak for three-quarters of an hour, in which case you should, keep to agreed upon time limits or to what you believe your audience can not only tolerate, but also enjoy. Study other successful speeches you've heard or read, analyze the techniques that made them work, and adopt those that you can use productively. If you make a mistake, correct it—keep your concentration and avoid letting your mind drift. Watch your audience to see how they're responding, then adjust volume, pace, or detail as necessary: speak to them rather than at them. Be kind, be friendly, make your point, and sit down.

Points to Ponder

1. *Recall a successful speech you've heard or read: what made it work?* Write down *the reasons why you liked it and remembered it.*

2. *Here are the steps in an ancient speech format that scholars call a "Classical Oration." Think of a topic on which you may want or have to make a speech, then sketch out your points so that they fit this model. Even if you don't actually deliver the speech in that fashion, the practice of organizing the speech will help you with future cases. The model, whether you follow it or not, gives you a* starting point *from which to consider your current needs.*

Postscript on Small-Group Communication

Often in business one needs to work and speak in small groups rather in public forums or before large audiences. While *Beowulf* doesn't tell us a lot about small-group communication—beyond of course what we may apply from what we've already learned about public speaking—we may derive a few general rules. These rules follow philosopher Paul Grice's maxims for productive exchange:

1. Give enough information, but not too much.

2. Be honest.

3. Keep to the point.

4. Be clear, considerate, and brief.

From Beowulf's own conversations in the poem, we can add a couple other simple points to remember:

1. Give your opinions when your group want them.

2. Take care about when you must remain formal versus when you can speak more intimately.

Otherwise, remember what you learned about public speaking, and apply those rules judiciously.

22

The Value of Good Manners

I now wish to ask one boon, Prince of the Bright-Danes,
that I may alone cleanse Heorot.

(i.e., May I help you?)

The Idea

As we examined public speaking in the last chapter, you may have noticed that in *Beowulf* one of the typical aspects of successful speeches is good manners. In fact, proper, respectful behavior establishes the basis for successful interactions of all sorts. In *Beowulf* a person can't get by for very long without it. Sometimes we forget, in a time when we hate and break every rule we can, that we can't get along without good manners, either.

Our own age seems to have developed a scorn not only for good manners, but for civility of any sort, as though we viewed it as a sign of weakness or even senility. Today we more often begin interactions by suspecting rather than respecting others, and we assume that anyone who acts respectfully must want something from us that we really don't want to give. But good manners need not imply subservience or social hierarchy; a code of behavior simply allows us a degree of comfort when we meet to interact, because for each interaction we know how to show respect to others and accept the respect they show us.

In the past good manners, at their best, facilitated interactions to make them beneficial to both or all parties. Of course many cultures used some notions of manners to express and enforce the subservience of one group to another, either by class, race, gender, or nation, a practice most of us would agree is inherently bad. That's probably why our nominally egalitarian culture has come to reject manners of any sort, though the oppression of past ages may now be more an excuse than a reason in a society obsessively self-conscious and dedicated to self-image and self-promotion.

Beowulf isn't a sentimental poem, and it doesn't presume romantic notions about human nature. The poet knew a world of violence, horror, and blood and recognized that sometimes people just take what they want by force. But such actions usually, in the long run, have dire consequences: they initiate acts of vengeance or even blood-feuds that last for generations. The poem shows that if you want something, you do best to recruit allies, even if that just means acquiring their permission to attempt to do them a favor, particularly if you want to do it on their own soil. Aggression leads to more aggression, while respectful behavior begets allegiances and peace. We can learn a lot from that assumption.

"Good manners" in *Beowulf* doesn't imply *chivalry*. Chivalry came into being, if anyone ever really practiced it, much later, largely as a literary phenomenon, derived from the equestrian practices and the general military and social training of knights to serve their lords and, as they understood it then, to serve God. In *Beowulf* the "code" has to do with knowing what to say and how to say it in specific social situations. Besides the thief who steals the cup from the dragon, we don't really meet anyone in the poem of other than the warrior/ruling class, so what we learn dictates how such persons should speak to one another and treat one another to consolidate friendship, peace, and mutual prosperity—a pretty good plan for businesses to follow as well.

Specifically the code of behavior reduces to a few basic maxims, which follow.

1. When you want to enter foreign territory or to undertake a task not normally directly within your purview, appear openly before the appropriate authority and ask permission. You're likely to prevent a battle by doing so. Show respect to senior officials, but don't neglect expressing thanks to others who have helped you.

2. In a contest, even an insult match, or when you decide to have a joke at another person's expense, always allow your opponent room to save face. Otherwise, prepare for the battle you're likely to face yourself.

3. Eat and drink joyfully with benefactors and followers, but avoid excesses that can sap your strength, mental or physical.

4. Treat not only your host, but also your host's family with respect.

5. When you fight, fight fairly. Expect someone from your opponent's faction to seek vengeance anyway.

6. Accept gifts graciously. Give them even more graciously and at every opportunity.

7. Give compliments as often, generously,
    and publicly as you can without com-
    promising truth or your honor.

8. Even when someone fails you, avoid
    embarrassing him or her. Focus on your
    responsibilities instead.

9. When you speak, mean what you say.
    Fulfill your boasts, and fulfill the loyal-
    ties you've vowed.

That list obviously omits a number of the points we often think
of when we consider manners: table etiquette, proper dress,
meeting the opposite sex. *Beowulf*'s concerns don't draw us
into those questions because it deals with issues that to the
Anglo-Saxon audience had far greater importance: living and
acting well, behaving courageously and heroically, maintaining loyalties, winning fame and glory. Those ideas give us a
fair sense, though, of what people thought really important
then, which we can compare valuably with those things we
find really important now.

The Passage

The first point above addresses Beowulf's arrival in Denmark
and his request that Hrothgar grant him permission to fight
Grendel in the manner he pleases. By fighting the monster
himself he takes away the opportunity for any of the Danish
warriors to win glory in the task, so he does right to ask their
lord first. Beowulf treats the coast guard, a man of lower status
than he has, respectfully when he arrives and when he leaves,
clarifying from his first arrival on Danish shores where he
comes from, what he wants, and that he intends only good
toward the Danes.

The second point derives largely from the brief insult match between Beowulf and Hunferth. Hunferth introduces the contest by asking Beowulf if he's the one who lost to Breca: that allows Beowulf to respond, saving face. Beowulf, however, not only refutes Hunferth's claim, but accuses him of fratricide—not very good manners on Beowulf's part, but then he does have to impress Hrothgar sufficiently to win his boon, and he never does fail to do his best to win unequivocally in a contest of any sort. Beowulf thus risks retribution from Hunferth, which of course he doesn't fear, knowing the other man far his inferior. Most important, though, is that when Hunferth makes a gesture to establish peace between them, Beowulf accepts immediately and makes a point to respond with ameliorative gestures of his own: praising the other man's sword and offering him his own should he die in battle.

Third, the Germanic folk attached a great deal of social significance to eating and drinking together, so a leader does well to offer extensive, pleasing feasts, and a soldier or guest does well to use such occasions to establish bonds of friendship and mutual loyalty. Beowulf feasts with the Danes before he fights for them.

Fourth, before he leaves Denmark Beowulf shows his respect to the queen—and to her sons—by honoring her request to support her sons at need: they're welcome, he says, to fosterage at Hygelac's court, a generous offer. Showing respect to his family confirms and deepens the friendship Beowulf has established with the king.

To exemplify the fifth point we need look no further than Beowulf's wish to fight Grendel—or any enemy he can—without weapons. Greater honor comes from a fair fight, but also we get a sense that for Beowulf fairness is in itself an important part of a laudable character, part of how one treats others—even monsters.

Sixth, gift exchange formed the basis of relations in the ancient Germanic world: treasures were for sharing, as when Hrothgar liberally rewards Beowulf for his victories, and Beowulf just as happily turns over all those gifts to Hygelac and his family. A person glories in receiving them and appreciates them mightily, but then one resists clinging to them. The hero as willingly gives away the precious gifts as he joyfully accepts them. The point, as we often say today, is in the giving—though showing pleasure at the receipt is also essential to good relationships.

The society in Beowulf is built nearly as much on public honor as on gift-giving, so Hrothgar honors Beowulf with words both before and after he heaps on the treasures. This seventh point shows the essential value in the poem of words as well as deeds. As soon as he finds the Geats on the Danish shore, the coast guard warns them, but also compliments their leader. Beowulf praises Hunferth's sword even though the weapon fails him: praising the weapon also praises the one who owns it.

Before he dies, the hero-king commends himself to his people, even to those soldiers who failed him at need—which takes us to point eight: anyone can get into a situation beyond his or her abilities, so we do best to forgive failure, or at least not dwell upon it, rather than to try to humiliate those who have failed. Humiliation only produces additional failure, because it breaks any hope of maintaining bonds that had previously held a relationship together. Beowulf's people will still have to fight for themselves after he's gone, so he does best to encourage them to that task rather than to brand them as failures or cowards, particularly because nearly anyone would have failed against the enemy they fled. We do best to think about the consequences of our words rather than to allow self-indulgence in pointless disparagement.

Finally, since words as well as deeds have importance—after all, they create the situation in which the deeds may occur—one does best not to speak lightly. Hunferth accuses Beowulf of not fulfilling a boast. The Danes don't fully trust Beowulf's boast to fight Grendel without weapons until he wins.

However, to medieval Germanic society the boast played an important point in the success of the soldier, rather as it does in some forms of billiards: you have to call the pocket for the shot to count, and for the soldier, the boast showed that the subsequent deed took courage and planning, rather than that it just happened by accident. Brave deeds win honor; accident doesn't. Further, proclaiming loyalty is closely related to boasting: one vows to fulfill at all costs the terms of a relationship. One shouldn't form them lightly, and as the poet shows, honor requires that, having made them, one fulfill them. That point applies to kings as well as to everyone all the way down the social scale. Kings must vow generosity and good leadership to their followers, and the followers must vow defense, respect, and honorable behavior to their king. People who break their word dissolve the bonds that keep the society functional and, as nearly as anything can in such a world, peaceful.

The Application

The specifics of good manners vary from age to age and culture to culture. Earlier generations ate with their fingers and tossed the bones behind them. In some cultures diners must clean their plates to show that they enjoyed the food, while in others they must leave some on the plate to show that their host was so generous as to serve more than enough.

The important application for us comes in our recognizing that manners have a place in successful social interaction: visitors must do their best to brief themselves on the manners of hosts, while hosts do well at least to know, so as to avoid offending against, cultural norms of valued guests.

The main point of good manners in our time isn't how to wield a dessert fork or by what honorific to address an ambassador's spouse—unless you happen to find yourself in such formal situations—but rather to show respect for other persons so as to facilitate successful interactions and create good relationships. That's really what good manners always meant, despite their misuse by oppressive parties.

If you know what a social situation demands of you, and you can perform your social duties with comfort and ease, you will not only feel more relaxed yourself and thus find yourself in a position to accomplish more, but you will put others at ease—and they'll love you and remember you for that.

Many of the beowulfian tenets of good manners still hold true. When you don't know if you may or should do something you'd like to do, ask permission. Some persons bent on personal success may tell you that's a waste of time and shows weakness. "Take what you want!" they say—I read it recently in a famous self-help/plan-for-success book. In some instances, such as in high-pressure sales jobs, that may often work. In the society of *Beowulf* it would have got you killed. But then that wasn't a society based on sales, as some will tell you ours is. You have to do your homework and know the difference. You must also look at what you mean by success.

If you're trying to sell the largest number of insurance policies or lawnmowers or golf clubs or used cars or bottles of perfume that you can, you may have success with more cajoling, energetic tactics. On the other hand, who doesn't appreciate a courteous salesperson who says "May I help you?" and really means it, someone who's there if you want him or her with information and a smile but out of the way if all you want to do is look?

Treat other creatures respectfully. Compliment others' successes. Compete within the rules, within the law, and within the bounds of decency. Share a meal. Share your experiences. Live up to your promises. Avoid making sarcastic comments or derogatory jokes at someone else's expense just to feed your ego. Build alliances with trust and hard work. Be wary of schemes and schemers: let actions win your trust, and take your time in giving that trust. If you must give it, others must earn it.

By rushing and screaming ourselves to near mania, we've ignored that success that lasts over time comes most dependably by our forming and respecting alliances, partnership, and friendships, treating supervisors, employees, customers, and even competitors honestly and honorably: that's one of the most important points we can learn from *Beowulf* for application in the present world. Today even more than in the past individual success requires interaction with many persons at many levels. You're not likely to fight Grendel alone; win allies with honorable behavior and good manners—whatever you determine them to be.

The Manager's Spotlight

History and current events have shown us innumerable examples of persons who gain wealth and power by abusing subordinates and colleagues. Most will brag about it, and many will even preach it. What we typically fail to consider is how much better they would have done acting more honorably and generously, not only for themselves but for those with them and after them to whom they owed a debt they seldom paid. Yes, you may succeed by intimidation. But you'd better be willing—and able—to keep intimidating, since when that ability fails, if that's all you've built on, you'll fall.

I'm aiming at something larger than the cliche "you can catch more flies with honey than with vinegar." There's some truth in that, but it turns good manners into a means to use others rather than to show respect for them and work with them. And besides, who wants flies anyway? Success requires attracting healthy allies, not pests.

Learn what people in your field and in your sphere of influence consider good manners. If you can do so honorably, without abusing yourself or others, practice them. If you find that you can't, you're probably in the wrong company or the wrong field. You need compatriots who can respect you and who can earn your respect not just by winning, but through quality of character.

Someone once asked baseball legend Ty Cobb, notably pugnacious in a time in which our society ignored in its heroes such traits as sadism and racism, how he felt about the life he'd lived. He replied that if he could do it all over again, he'd like to have had more friends.

Winning is fleeting. Look how long Beowulf gets to enjoy his victory over Grendel: one night. Then he must win again, and later again and again and again.

Good character remains. We show it through mutual respect. We show it, not exclusively, but at least initially, through good manners. Then, to the degree that we can, we live by it.

Having done so to the best of our ability, we've succeeded.

Points to Ponder

1. *What elements of "good manners" do you typically practice? Which would you like to practice? Which do you dismiss—and why do you dismiss them?*

2. *When you watch others practice good manners, do you usually appreciate or doubt their sincerity? Why?*

3. *What habits can you develop that will help you better show respect for others so that you may more easily acquire professional allies?*

23

A Sense of Irony

Too few defenders thronged to the king in his time of need.

(i.e., Keep your patience.)

The Idea

Many books, speakers, teachers, and managers extol the virtue of keeping a sense of humor.

Beowulf would amend that advice just slightly: for a sense of humor the poet would substitute a sense of *irony*. The poet doesn't recommend telling jokes, but remembering the absurdities of life.

Irony is one of those words that everyone hears, but few know exactly what it means. You know it when you hear it, but you don't necessarily know how to explain it. Don't let that worry you: even many dictionaries don't do a very good job of it because it's a difficult word to define. If you look it up, you'll find something like "an expression that means the opposite of what it seems to mean" or "an incongruity that casts a deliberate contrast between what the speaker says and what he or she means."

Those are pretty darn good definitions, but they lack anything of the *purpose* and the *feeling* that go with irony. We use irony typically to express a sad but humorous peculiarity of life: "things should work *so*, but because we often do stupid things, they tend to work out *so*."

Irony is somewhat like but not the same as sarcasm or satire. Sarcasm has as its purpose to mock someone. Irony may do that, or it may not. More typically irony is a shared recognition of something ridiculous rather than an attempt to make someone look ridiculous. Satire is lampooning something with the goal of changing it. Satire may use irony as one of its methods. But irony in itself doesn't aim to produce a change. It simply identifies a problematic incongruity.

Let's try an example. It's ironic that often politicians in attacking opponents will often proclaim them liars, while actually lying about or grossly exaggerating their own claim. We can talk sarcastically about a politician who does that or we can construct a satire to attempt to change such political behavior, but the shared recognition of the incongruity—how the speech and the action contradict each other—is the experience of irony. The sad part is that we believe we can do little to change something that appears to be part of the nature of political discourse. The funny part is that when we notice the incongruity, the politicians look stupid, and so do those members of the public who don't notice the abusers' abuses. The ironic commentator would, hearing the politician's statement and knowing his or her own lies, say something like this: "Thank God he's not lying!" The fact that he is lying, which the speaker has uncovered, is at once funny because of its revelation and sad because of its circumstances.

Well, you may say, what good does irony accomplish, then, if it doesn't set out to solve the problem and correct the abuses of the world? The Anglo-Saxons, like most peoples, recognized that we humans are flawed creatures and the world is often a vale of sorrows and tears. Sickness, pain, suffering, and death will trouble us no matter what we do, regardless of our powers, skills, and victories. Some things we can change, others we can't—though which is which may vary from person to person. For those things we can change, we apply our powers and skills with hope of victory. For those things we can't change, we have irony. Like Blues or chocolate or yoga, irony is a way to deal with the loss and silliness and suffering that the world inflicts on us without eliminating the causes.

These days, when we have science and technology to search out solutions for problems, and when some people believe that prayer can bring them the answers they need—solutions not available to pre-scientific peoples or those not fully converted to a religion, such as Christianity, that teaches that God answers them—we've tended to lose some of the appreciation of irony that *Beowulf* instills. We wonder: maybe I can live forever; maybe a drug can remove my pain; maybe a computer dating service can relieve my loneliness. The Anglo-Saxons looked at problems beyond their ken and found humor in them, both in the problem and in their inability to solve them. They also found consolation in the shared recognition of the perhaps impossible difficulty of the problem: at least everybody shared it, and so all could attempt to deal with it bravely.

But irony doesn't require insoluble problems. It requires only that we recognize the sad absurdity and share a chuckle over it. The ability to laugh together builds bonds, and, ironically, those bonds can sometimes help solve the problem that created the irony to begin with. Ironic, isn't it?

That's where we go back to the didactic purpose of *Beowulf*, that is, the poet's intention that we learn something from the text. The ironies in *Beowulf* do point to pretty universal human problems, some of which we may be able to affect, and others that still lie beyond our powers. Yet, in recognizing them together, we can better appreciate one another, since regardless of how we feel about life, we're all in it together.

Here are the false notions that *Beowulf* treats with irony: that people will appreciate heroism and learn from it; that heroism brings praise, appreciation, and immortality; that we can live without heroism; that the situation is always worse for us than it is for others; that people won't see our flaws if we point out theirs; that we can count on those we've put in positions of power to take care of us.

We could just as well treat those ideas ironically today.

While the danger of the ironic eye is that it may descend into peevish cynicism, the advantage is that it can keep a person from being too easily hoodwinked. Clear vision and resistance to cant and unbridled enthusiasm are necessary for continued success.

The Passage

We can say that the poet enveloped the whole poem in irony: it's about a hero who braves death to slay monsters, but *Beowulf* begins and ends with the funerals of hero-kings.

Other ironies come into play with the funerals. When Scyld Scefing died, his people gave him a funeral at sea: they set his body, surrounded by treasure, in a ship and pushed it off into the waves to float where it would. "Not one of the wise men, heroes under heaven, knew who received that cargo," the poet remarks coolly. Scyld came to the Danes out of nowhere, built them into a powerful nation, and returned into nowhere, nor could any sort of heroism, even fame and glory, prevent that end. Similarly, when Beowulf dies, the people bury with his ashes the treasures he won for them. Why? They waste them because they want to honor their king and don't feel worthy of keeping them. And Beowulf has saved them, but for what? For invasion by hostile neighbors who have been waiting for their chance.

That fact raises another irony. Wiglaf suggests that Beowulf erred in fighting the dragon, that he should have remained alive to protect the Geats from those dangerous neighbors.

But Beowulf had to die eventually anyway, which would have left the Geats in the same position: needing to fend for themselves. At least in the meantime he dispatches a certain and immediate enemy. Worse yet: the soldiers he trusts most fail him at need despite his many kindnesses to them.

Even if you're Beowulf, the greatest hero of your age, you can't please all the people all the time, nor can you count on those for whom you sacrifice, though you give your life for them— that's the irony of ironies.

When Hunferth accuses Beowulf of failing to achieve his boast against Breca, he sets up for Beowulf the perfect ironic comeback: how can Hunferth criticize another soldier when he hasn't fulfilled his own duty to protect his king and people from attackers? That problem always haunts would-be critics: if you can't do the job, how can you find fault with others' performance? Hunferth points out what may or may not have been an imperfect success of Beowulf's while ignoring a gross fault of his own. The sad thing, the ironic thing: we do it all the time. More ironic yet: we *must* do it. We learn partly by finding what's wrong and trying to fix it, by making errors so that we identify, and thereby learn to transcend, our limitations, if we're lucky enough to get a chance.

Early in the poem, when first we learn about Grendel's monstrous behavior, the poet says that after feasting and drinking, the Danish soldiers fell asleep in their hall. "They knew then no sorrow, that misery of men," even as the savage monster lurks outside, waiting to burst in upon them and consume thirty at a time. The unconscious soldiers know no sorrow only because they've drunk themselves into oblivion, unaware that they're about to be eaten. The world, the poet shows us, in case we hadn't noticed, is a dangerous place. Inattention to danger doesn't eliminate its presence. You may briefly, but not indefinitely, escape the monster by hiding under the bed.

Then again, life isn't necessarily so easy for the monster, either, especially if a Beowulf happens to come along. When Grendel pulls away from Beowulf, feeling his arm ripped out at the shoulder, he runs off in pain and panic. Yet "not so easy is it to flee, try it he who will," says the poet. "One must eventually meet that place where the body sleeps in death, the fast after the feast." Like the soldiers on whom he feeds, the monster, too, must face the fear of death. All who feast someday confront the long fast that follows. The monster suffers the same end as the rest of us.

Very funny, no doubt. The poet isn't trying to make us laugh, but to get us to see the absurdities of some of our misconceptions about life. Interesting that some people who don't even read *Beowulf* will reject it because they believe it's mere fantasy, and therefore not worth their time. *Beowulf* is in many ways as true and honest a piece of writing as you'll find. In these days we tend to associate truth and honesty with political exposés or with some celebrity publicly confessing a menu of overindulgences. The value of truth and honesty in writing is that it dispatches sentimentality and illuminates understandings that make our lives better, that help us to live fuller and more aware lives.

The ironies in *Beowulf* keep us fully aware of human limitations and failings while showing us those traits we can cultivate to minimize their ill effects and maximize our strengths. What could be more helpful and come closer to truth than that?

The Application

A sense of irony goes a long way toward helping us accept, understand, and then deal with our problems. Irony isn't the same thing as cynicism or despair; it recognizes the problems into which we get ourselves, laughs at our foolishness in doing so, and suggests that we had better get busy and solve them if we can, accept and deal with them if we can't.

The irony in *Beowulf* reminds us to avoid sentimentality, that life will always swing us from happiness to sorrow, back again, then back again, that life takes us on strange, winding, fascinating, dangerous paths, so we'd better keep our wits about us. Fortunes change, and mortality binds us all. Even as you accept kudos for a job well done, you must continue to prepare for the next one. Regardless of how well you've served your customers today, how carefully you've attended to clients today, how much your students have learned today, you can't assume they'll remain loyal to you tomorrow. The irreplaceable joys of today may linger into tomorrow, or they may depart never to return, and some sort of monster will eventually catch up to you, whether a cold virus or a temporarily unbeatable competitor or the Grim Reaper himself.

If you can enjoy the day, do your best to achieve the small or large victories available to you, and laugh at all the foolishness that lies beyond your ability to repair, you've learned one of the most important lessons of *Beowulf*. Of course, the accompanying story teaches us to stretch ourselves, to find our limits and maybe on one great occasion even to surpass them—while knowing that decline must follow. As Browning's Pippa says, your reach should exceed your grasp, or what's a heaven for? Beowulf does that, too.

In the great Hindu epic *Bhagavad-Gita*, the hero Arjuna learns from Krishna, an incarnation of God on earth, to do his duty, achieve what he can, live in the *process*, and detach himself from the specific results. If you fixate on the results, you'll fail in the process. If Beowulf were to fix his attention on defeating Grendel rather than on what he must do in the heat of the moment, he would probably be killed. If Beowulf were to fix his consciousness on the defeat of the dragon rather than on what he must do in the battle to defeat the dragon, he would not only die, but fail to kill the dragon, a disaster for his folk beyond the disaster imminent for himself.

The irony is that the best way to win is to forget about winning and concentrate on the process.

Yes, you can sometimes will yourself to greater performance, even to victory. But you win by willing the performance, not by looking past it to the result.

The irony is that, win or lose, other people may appreciate you or not. Accomplish herculean deeds, and people may remember you, or they may not.

After he'd retired from baseball, Mickey Mantle used to stand by the window during a storm to listen to the rain pelt against the window glass: the sound reminded him of the applause he'd known as a player. As any great athlete—or an achiever in any profession—is almost a force of nature, as wonderful as a mountain or a storm, so any force of nature will eventually blow itself out or simply wear away. And for all that we strive, sweat, strain, compete, connive, contend.

Pretty silly, but that's who we are as a species. If we do it in good spirit, with generosity, even magnanimity—and an eye for the irony—we can at least make the most of the ride for as long as it lasts.

The Manager's Spotlight

Any manager, parent, teacher, anyone dedicated to one's own or to others' success, must inevitably face a lifetime of excuses. The best way to deal with them is to treat them with a little irony.

That person who fumes, "I don't want any excuses; I just want success!" unless he or she is using such a statement for motivational purposes (which probably won't work), is acting both unrealistically and egotistically. Separating "excuse" and "reason" is a difficult matter, one a manager must often undertake, since your people—and you—will often fall short of complete success. We overuse the word fail. Many people are so afraid of failing that they'll never succeed, because they can't muster the will to try.

You must be scrupulous with yourself: are you making excuses or are you finding the reasons why things haven't worked out as you wished? If you find reasons, you can perhaps enhance performance and improve or else realize you'd do better to spend your energies elsewhere.

With others, tune up your sense of irony. You'll learn some good reasons for why individuals succeed or fail, and you'll hear every excuse in the book, many of them outright hilarious. Be generous and forgive when you can, be firm and exacting when you must, but separate yourself from the excuses and the persons who make them: if you can do that, you'll save yourself a lot of suffering, and by staying calm you'll more easily reach rational solutions or decisions that may get you past the excuses to success on the next try.

Points to Ponder

1. *Think of the last time you made an excuse, or explained the reason, for less than optimal performance. If you were honest with yourself, how can you avoid the hindrance in the future? If you weren't, consider how understanding the problem ironically—in the context of general human shortcomings—can help you change your attitude toward similar instances that may lie ahead of you.*

2. *Recall the last time someone gave you a reason, or an excuse, for failing you in some way: did you try to distinguish between reason and excuse, to understand and deal with the situation, or did you get angry? Consider if dealing with the problem ironically could have helped you keep a clear head and get past the problem rather than dwelling on it.*

3. *Consider: with what sorts of problems can ironic humor help, and with what sort may it actually exacerbate the problem?*

24

Family

Rewards depend entirely on you:
I have few close kinsmen but you, Hygelac.

(i.e., Remember your family.)

The Idea

Family plays an enormous part in how *Beowulf* works as a story and in how it achieves emotional affects on the reader. Few elements in our own lives have greater importance than the life we share with our families.

Especially in past ages family determined most of a person's prospects, from livelihood to political alliances to marriage partner. Family determined class, trade, affiliations, all the way to what happened to a person's body after death.

In some ways, though nominally we have more freedoms, many influences of family ties haven't changed all that much.

Genetic predisposition determines our potentials, and family affiliations normally influence the kind of education and opportunities that arise at least early in our lives. Unless one is orphaned young, family create the environment in which we begin to grow into our adult selves, whether we react by wishing to turn out like them or to become something different than what we see in them. Even most people whom fortune separates from their families long to learn something of them and may spend years tracking down information about them.

As we mature and find our places in the world, family again at least influences and often determines our identity and our activities. If we marry and have children, we extend our families further, articulating our lives with a larger and more diverse group of people through and perhaps beyond our community. If we're lucky, through our lives we make friends who become to us as though they were family, and their families and ours mix, extending our mutual influences.

With family comes purpose, connection, continuity. With family comes responsibility. Most of us, if someone were to ask why we work at our jobs, would give as one of the reasons "to help take care of my family." Particularly if you are the sole breadwinner, though these days even if you work just to supplement family income, you can probably say "my family couldn't get along without my paycheck," and regardless of how much you like your job, you stick to it at least in part out of a sense of obligation.

In our time, more than in any other time in the past, more of us (though by no means yet everyone) can choose our work, or we can choose a new line of work, based on preference: that is a great boon. Often even if we choose badly, we may get more education and eventually choose again. More of us have come to expect some sort of personal satisfaction from work. That desire has sometimes helped, sometimes hindered, our ability to gain satisfaction from family life. The possibility of seeking better work has driven us to educate our children to increase for them the probability of seeking and finding a career that not only pays for their needs, but that they also find fulfilling. The joys, sorrows, and responsibilities of working life spill over into family life. In cases of those who run family businesses, the two may coalesce inseparably.

In the world of *Beowulf* family determines status and work, establishes social networks breakable only by crime, and imposes lifelong responsibilities.

Occasionally someone such as Scyld Scefing appears out of the mists and rises to power, but such characters, few and mythic, represent the exception: they show that exceptional persons can achieve incredible results, and extraordinary deeds can accomplish amazing ends, but only if some family proves kind enough to give the orphaned, exiled, or disenfranchised person a home and a chance.

For the most part the idea of family in *Beowulf* explores the tensions between individual achievement or power and family responsibilities. The individual person must live up to the best qualities that the society prescribes for his or her class and family, and he or she must plan for and act according to the needs of the family. All of Old English poetry bemoans the fate of the poor person exiled from family and country. *Beowulf* particularly extols the virtues of those who love and care for their families and who prepare the next generation for not only survival, but also success; it bemoans the fates of those who make poor choices or fail to support their families at need.

The Passage

Beowulf goes to Denmark against the advice (but not the order) of his uncle, King Hygelac, partly to gain experience as a soldier and to win fame and glory, but also to pay back a debt that his family acquired when King Hrothgar of Denmark helped his father, Ecgtheow, in a time of need, when he was facing exile for killing another man in combat.

Sometimes readers wonder why Beowulf shows what seems to them disloyalty to his uncle and king by, seemingly, not following his wishes. That problem has several solutions, each important to what the poem can teach us. First, the individual must have some freedom to steer his own course—in that time men had a little freedom, women very little, but both had to exercise what freedom they had to accomplish what good they could. Beowulf knows that as a hero, he must test himself. Fame and glory give him what immortality his world provides, but they also help his king: a king with great heroes at his side faced a greatly reduced likelihood of attacks from other tribes or treachery from within. Second, we do find in Beowulf a bit of the comic-book hero: he intends to fight and destroy evil and chaos where he finds them—though only with the permission of those who have authority over the territory in which he intends to fight, and he has no designs whatever on their lands or possessions or ideologies. Third, and most important for this chapter, he goes to Denmark, as we have discussed before, to pay back a family debt. He does a good turn, a monstrously good turn, for the man who helped his father. Furthermore, he offers to do what he can to help Hrothgar's sons. An obligation creates a *family bond*: what you do for a member of my family you do for me, what you do to a member of my family you do to me. You treat me well, my whole family will do their best to return the kindness; you treat me violently, my whole family joins the blood-feud.

The warrior bands were more like families than militias: they ate together, drank together, told stories together, and shared gifts regularly. They operated much like a family unit. They pledged a loyalty as thick as blood to defend one another.

I'm not recommending blood-feud. *Beowulf*, though, encourages its audience to see family as an extension of the individual and an individual as a limb of the family. Through family we stretch back to the beginning of time and forward into an otherwise uncontrollable future.

The fact that Hrothgar has no heroes at hand sufficient to manage Grendel says something about his family, too: though they come from the line of the great Scyld, their blood is beginning to fail. They remain good leaders, but without the inherent heroism of previous ages, and even as leaders they will fall in the generations to come. Still, they can accomplish a lot: they can remain good and true to their families and people, generous toward and appreciative of guests and benefactors, and attentive to the troubles ahead. Hrothgar's queen, Wealhtheow, reminds Hrothgar of his obligations to his sons, not to think about appointing Beowulf his heir, and she hints to Beowulf that he shouldn't try to disrupt that obligation. Beowulf understands her point, and, despite the fact that he has saved them from horror and perhaps extinction, before he leaves he assures the Danes that he has no interest in taking over their country. He has achieved his goals and fulfilled his familial obligation, and so he goes home.

When Beowulf returns to Geatland, he gives Hygelac important gifts: even more than the treasures that he won, which he turns over to his king, he returns a hero more prepared than ever to defend king and country. By the time Beowulf himself becomes king, his reputation has grown sufficiently that, even once he has aged, no one will attack his people—in Beowulf's time, a hero could give king and family no greater gift.

Further, when Hygelac dies in battle, the queen offers Beowulf the throne, but he doesn't accept: he supports the claim of Hygelac's sons, and he serves them, his cousins, as hero, just as he did their father. Beowulf understands the importance in his world of order based in family, and he won't intrude on what he considers proper succession.

"Fate has lured away all my kin, according to the Master's decree. Now I must go after them," says Beowulf with his final breath. When Beowulf dies, he has no son to take his place, a rather grave failing, since the poet has taught us through the story of Scyld and his descendants that among the tasks of a good king, one must have an heir—best of all a heroic one—to assure smooth succession. But Beowulf does the next best thing: having killed the dragon that threatens his people, he appoints Wiglaf, his closest kinsman and the best hero available to the people, to take his place. Wiglaf, while no Beowulf, will honorably rule and defend his people, aiming to fulfill his familial obligation as he does by joining Beowulf in the fight against the dragon.

Family in *Beowulf* is about continuity, but also about showing respect and love for one's ancestors and providing safety and opportunity for one's descendants.

The Application

The characters of *Beowulf* don't fixate on success in the same way we often do today: to them *success* means surviving in a harsh and dangerous world. *Thriving* means acquiring the ability to pursue honor, to assure their families and peoples safety in the present, and to offer a worthy legacy to the next generation. As we often do today, they crave fame—at least the heroes do—and fear infamy, since in their world immortality comes only when later generations remember them and speak well of them. The best of them don't seek political power; they support power that keeps the people safe and treats them justly and generously. They value treasures and gifts, not for monetary value, but because of the honor that accompanies them, and because they can pass that honor along from one person to another or one generation to another as the treasures become heirlooms (as the word *heir-loom*, Old English *heir lome*, a tool passed on to an heir, itself denotes). The fame that they win honors their families, and the honor that they win disseminates among their family members.

Family implies *obligation*, but the Old World saw that obligation not as a burden, rather as the process of living. In regions not dominated by monotheism, that was one's reason for living: the affiliation and continuity of family bonds.

Along with birth and death, we share that connection with them. I'm not even sure that they saw love in the same way we do. In English but one word has descended to describe the many sorts of love we experience and express: for spouse, for parents, for siblings, for a dear friend, for a favorite activity or food. The Greeks had half a dozen words to distinguish those feelings. Plato in his book *The Republic* suggests that living in families may *not* always be good for us—the Spartans experimented with that idea. But most human cultures have seen love and family—and perhaps honor—as the driving forces behind our work, what today has evolved into our idea of the *career*.

I don't know if we still believe in honor in the old way. We use the term in contexts, particularly military or athletic, occasionally academic. I don't hear it often in the context of business, and I hear it less and less often with anything more than empty sarcasm in the realm of leadership.

I think we do still believe in family, even if our notions of the family unit and how it does or should work continue to evolve. Some people ascribe our contemporary social failings to our faltering willingness or ability to commit to the traditional notion of the nuclear family. However we as individuals conceive it, the draw toward familial affiliation drives us. Even if we feel alone, live alone, or work alone, the desire for the "familiar," the association with colleagues in a company or like enthusiasts in a hobby, the remembrance of "auld acquaintance," companionable sharing of food and drinks, the longing we experience far in advance of holidays, the detached excitement of computer chatrooms, even if we're too shy to take the actual steps ourselves, irresistible nebulous impulses move us to maintain the groups we have or to want to form new ones that give us some stay against the immense notion of eternity and the dark doubts it inspires.

Whether business busts and finances fizzle, or markets boom careers soar, our last thoughts at the end of the day return, as they do for Beowulf, to our families, where we find them trouble our dreams or bring rest to our sleep.

The Manager's Spotlight

Despite that admirable devotion to your job, remember that both you and your employees have families and that your main reasons for being on the job may have as much to do with them as with anything else.

Work hard, and expect hard work from your charges, but know that you must respect limits: your ability and theirs to provide for and enjoy your families takes precedence over trivial daily chores. You may expect extraordinary devotion occasionally; you may not make it standard procedure without offending the essence of human experience: other persons' lives aren't about you.

For those readers who have for one or another tragic reason lost your families: I have no words sufficient to express my sorrow or wise enough to console you. I hope you find solace in friends, clubs, work, and recreations. I hope where you haven't blood or marital ties, you have other affiliations that offer a stay against the loneliness of the world. But even you have an obligation to respect the familiar pleasures and obligations of your co-workers. Beowulf makes that point as one of its most important themes.

Points to Ponder

1. Recall when you were sixteen years old; list the five aspects of your life that were most important to you then. Next, list the five aspects that have greatest importance to you now. Then list the five points that will probably have the greatest value to you ten years from now. Examine the list and your reasons for the items you included.

2. Think of the closest (in terms of relationships) families you know; what keeps them close? Think of the most distant families you know; what keeps them apart? Think of the companies you know that are most and least like families; what policies or behaviors make them so? Consider the traits that you distill from such an analysis: which of them lead to success and which detract from it?

25

Unmaking the Myths

Each of us must know the end of life in the world—win glory before death he who can!

(i.e., We must all die—but maybe not just yet.)

The Myths

Particularly these days, when we've wrapped ourselves in notions of inherent self-worth, self-actualization, and self-fulfillment, many of us enter the work world profoundly weighed down with myths about what we'll find there, how things do and should work, and what we'll accomplish. Our preconceptions come not merely from childhood fantasies, but also from the prevailing myths of our culture, with sources from the left over resonances of George Washington and Horatio Alger to the latest "reality" television and, yes, self-help book. To set and accomplish goals apt for us and to build successful, rewarding lives, we must sift through the myths to find out what the myths mean. Myths are stories about the nature of truth, not factual truths in themselves.

Some readers have looked at *Beowulf* as myth, but it isn't really myth, nor is it legend. It's an epic poem with a symbolic story designed by the poet to communicate ideas in such a way as to move audiences to consider those ideas and perhaps adopt them to live better.

Among the other productive accomplishments we can derive from studying *Beowulf*, we can enumerate a list of what we may call "myths," but myths in the modern, ironic sense of *false stories*, that the poem explodes for us. If we pay attention, the poem directs our attention to a number of ideas that may help us approach the work world with clearer heads and a greater awareness of how the world works and how we may best, for a time, survive and prosper in it.

In this chapter I'll stray from the structure we've followed up to now so that one by one we can uncover some dangerous myths and begin to develop a sense of how, in the context of what we learn from *Beowulf*, we may deal with them.

Myth #1: Work should be fun, rewarding, fulfilling, and satisfying.

Just because a story or idea is mythic doesn't mean it can't come true. But in this case you'd better not accept a job expecting it to be full of fun and laughs, even if you do comedy for a living.

Work can sometimes be fun, rewarding, fulfilling, and satisfying, but often it isn't. Some jobs almost never are.

We call activities *work* because, if we do them right, they're hard. We call paid positions *jobs* because, regardless of what's good about them, they have elements we wouldn't do without being paid for them.

If you have the good fortune to enjoy your work and find it fulfilling on a regular basis, consider yourself lucky and blessed, and do your best to help your co-workers feel the same.

But more likely than not you'll find aspects of it that annoy, confound, or even offend you. That doesn't necessarily make you profoundly oppressed; it makes you like the vast majority of working persons.

We aim to find work in which the majority of the tasks are tolerable or better, and none of the tasks is intolerable. Then we try to make the job better. Or we seek another one.

While Beowulf probably feels excitement during his monster battles—the poet doesn't tell us one way or the other—and he certainly feels fulfilled by his victories, he definitely doesn't enjoy almost getting stabbed with Grendel's Mother's claws or getting scorched and poisoned by the dragon.

Myth #2: Everyone should aim for promotion; the main goal of accomplishment is to achieve a leadership position.

Not everyone is constitutionally suited for leadership, so not everyone should aim for it. You should migrate toward the position where the duties and rewards please you. While we do well to stretch ourselves, we need not feel obligated to accept a position for which we don't feel ready or that doesn't suit our talents simply because it bears a better title or pays more money or moves us to supervisory status.

On the other hand, don't allow undue self-doubt to bring you to turn down an opportunity that may offer great rewards if you want to try it and believe you can grow into it and succeed.

Beowulf is a hero, a soldier. When he first has the choice to accept kingship, he turns it down, even though Hrothgar has told him he'll make a good king one day, should the opportunity arise. He turns it down because he doesn't believe he has a right to it.

Later he accepts the kingship probably because no one else stands in line for it, and he knows that he has the best chance of anyone of succeeding in it. As king, he may decide to leave the dragon fight to others, but he knows that only he can hope to destroy the monster. He chooses tasks because they suit his skills, fall within his duties, or devolve naturally to him.

You need not choose as scrupulously as Beowulf, but neither need you accept a position you don't want just because it offers money and prestige.

Success means achievement, contribution, and happiness, not title.

Myth #3: We should court superiors' positive estimation of us.

That's a tough myth to dispel, because family, the educational system, and society in general preach it loudly and often. But it isn't entirely true according to *Beowulf*.

That's not to say that pleasing your superiors is bad. It's a matter of the order in which we proceed. To please them *by doing well* will, normally, help you advance and grow. But to do well you must first be true to yourself and your principles. Otherwise, you can never feel happy within your own skin and you can never reach your potential as a complete human being. That doesn't mean you should be insubordinate; it does mean that in the long run one succeeds better through accomplishment than by "kissing up."

We best please superiors—assuming they're worth pleasing—

by doing an extraordinary job with the tasks we undertake. If we set out to *court* them rather than simply to do a good job, we'll do less than our best work. Smart managers will know when you're aiming merely to impress or flatter them, and anyone who wants a sycophant rather than a productive employee won't reward your efforts, but will only exploit you and expect you to debase yourself further. Never give yourself away, professionally or personally, in the working world. Never give in to "high school politics" (yes, you'll still see that in the professional world). Your life, talents, and spirit are worth too much for that.

Beowulf goes to Denmark to fight Grendel even though Hygelac counsels him against it. Hygelac fears he'll lose his nephew, but Beowulf feels the need to prove himself, to test his abilities and acquire credentials. From his point of view he isn't foolhardy, because he knows he can succeed and believes he will. He accepts the risk. For another person that choice would be foolish; for Beowulf it's necessary. He doesn't court favor; he *wins* favor through his deeds, deeds true to his own nature.

Myth #4: Success means money, title, and perks.

We always have people tell us that money doesn't mean success, but most of them don't really believe it. Nonetheless, it's a myth.

Success means achievement, contribution, and happiness.

When Beowulf wins wealth, he gives it away. He never really wants a kingship, accepting it only when he has little choice and knows he can serve his people better by accepting it than by turning it down to remain a soldier. The text gives us no reason to believe that Beowulf uses his office to acquire any special perks or privileges. In fact, when the dragon appears, rather than try to protect himself so as to protect his office, he steps to the front and accepts the deadly duty to solve the problem himself.

History teaches us that while most of us spend a great deal of our energy seeking them, wealth and title don't bring happiness. They may or may not bring unhappiness.

Ah, that elusive notion, *happiness*, so much more complex than momentary pleasure. We talk about it all the time. Early literatures say little about it. It seems to come most often when we get to use our talents in activities that both require and reward our energies or when we experience the mutual love and admiration of family, friends, and colleagues.

Victory brings Beowulf joy, but even impending death doesn't bring him unhappiness. Only when he learns of the dragon's attack and fears that he has done something to provoke divine wrath do "dark thoughts well up in his breast," and only at the dragon's destruction does he express anger. He finds success, and we may guess happiness, in employing his abilities to useful purpose, glorious deeds for the general good.

Myth #5: As the child, so the man or woman.

We often make the mistake of passing judgment on a person early in his or her life, estimating abilities and potentials and writing off those persons who fail to show precocious excellence.

As a child Beowulf, we learn, was a "coalbiter," a male Cinderella who sits by the warm fire and shows no eagerness for danger or adventure. No one expected much of him. His talents emerge as he matures. The poet tells us he grows up to become the greatest hero of his time. When he dies, as the poem concludes, the people say of him that "of the kings of the world he was toward the people the mildest, gentlest, and kindest, and he was the most eager for praise" (though that last line may also mean "most eager *to praise others*"). In his battles Beowulf accomplishes what no one else can, as a person he remains true to his code of honor and his notion of goodness, and as a king he rules peacefully for fifty years—we can hardly expect more of a shy little boy than that.

We weigh down our children with intelligence tests, psychological tests, physical tests, then assume we can predict their lives by the results, and then we often place stress on them to live up to test results or restraints on them to live down to them. Testing itself isn't necessarily the problem, if it uncovers hidden talents the awareness of which may give a child a chance to develop unrecognized skills. Judging by means of tests alone is the problem: we may inhibit individuals from growing fully into themselves. Some children develop later than others and many, particularly if they aren't born to wealth and privilege, as Beowulf is, never get the opportunities to explore talents that may otherwise emerge as they mature.

We owe everyone that chance.

Myth #6: People at the top know what they're doing. Otherwise, they wouldn't be there.

Hrothgar, the poet tells us, is a good king, but he can do nothing about Grendel. Hygelac, too, is a "good king," but he conducts a disastrous raid among the Franks and Hugas that results in his own death and that of all his soldiers but one, Beowulf, who seems to have almost supernatural ability to survive—only the deadliest of monsters, a dragon, can bring Beowulf down. Those men largely succeed as kings, yet even they may confront problems they can't solve or make disastrous decisions that cause great loss and suffering. Even Beowulf, another good king, dies in a battle that some of his people, Wiglaf at least, think he shouldn't have undertaken alone.

We must never allow ourselves the romantic assumption that the people on top know what they're doing.

We must have the fortitude to insist that they prove it and that they keep us informed of failures as well as successes, plans as well as results.

Consider the large number of cases that have recently come to public light detailing incredible abuses by CEO's and other corporate leaders. Consider also the vast discrepancies between the salaries and benefits of upper-level managers and those of the other employees. The gulf looks more like the abuse of privilege by later monarchs than what we find in *Beowulf*, where wealth serves for gift-giving and greedy leaders are denigrated for their abuses rather than praised as models to which one should aspire.

The persons who work hard and intelligently to reach the top have earned our praise. We must then hold them to ethical standards to prevent the temptation to abuse the positions and powers they have won.

We may show honor, respect, and admiration. We must expect accountability and remain watchful.

Myth #7: Better technology means a better life.

Like most myths this one has a grain of truth, but it doesn't hold up in all circumstances. Better technology helps if we apply it better, but it doesn't replace virtues we need to survive and prosper.

Of greater importance is the quality of the person using the technology.

While we can't exactly call Beowulf a Luddite, the technology available to him doesn't always help him. He uses few weapons successfully: he has too much strength for anything less than an iron shield and a magic sword. He wins the Grendel battle because he has greater courage and composure. In the Grendel's Mother battle he uses a mail shirt, which protects him from her claws and water beasts, and he kills her with a magic sword that dissolves in her blood. Into the dragon fight he takes a large, iron shield, a sword, and a knife. The shield protects him briefly, and the sword breaks—only the lowest level of technology, plus his courage, strength, and commitment, as well as the help of a friend, works at the moment of truth.

We can say that the monsters have better natural weapons. The Grendel family are large, strong, fast, remorselessly murderous, impervious to most weapons, and armed with claws and fangs. The dragon has size, fire, poison, claws, the ability to fly, and a body covering of scales tougher than iron. Beowulf uses increasingly effective technology as the fights get more difficult, and the technology helps somewhat, but he wins not because of the technology, but because of his character: clarity, fortitude, tenacity, persistence, and devotion to duty produce the victory. That's why no one else carrying the same or even better weapons could have succeeded.

Beowulf prospers as king not because his people have better technology than potential enemies, but because they have a better and more intimidating leader. Yet Beowulf doesn't use his abilities to oppress neighbors, only to keep his people free of attack from them: the value of humanity trumps the lure of technology.

For us as for Beowulf, a better life doesn't necessarily follow better technology; it depends on the technology available to us and how we use it.

The Manager's Spotlight

Corporate (and political) myths, like clichés, may once have had some meaning or value, but over time they tend to become not only trite or banal, but dangerous. They lure us into false security and carelessness. Leaders and managers have an obligation not to rely on them just to reduce employees or customers to insensibility, and you have an equal obligation not to let superiors get away with them. Given the limits of secrecy with respect to proper marketplace competition, you can't let empty answers to urgent questions endanger employee or public interests: myths will catch up to you and swallow you, and anyone else around, eventually.

Beowulf, like so much of the great literature of the past, teaches about free will and responsibility. Readers who haven't read any of it often assume it teaches oppression and inequality, but it doesn't. We may, and perhaps must, levy the same charges against contemporary institutions, corporate, governmental, academic, or otherwise, and we must "read" them to find the answer: do they support freedom, compassion, and human achievement, or do they exploit labor, dupe the public, and enslave us to greed and private ambition?

At the beginning of the book I offered the warning that Beowulf is a moral, didactic poem. As I conclude the book, I reiterate the point. Today our leaders often make a sham of morality, ethics, and responsibility, claiming them as a way to seek public support, then using that support merely for personal gain. Your career may provide great personal gain without your failing on any of those counts. Your life is as important as anyone else's, and, depending on your choices, you need not feel obligated to live it in perpetual self-sacrifice.

But if you choose to lead, if you choose to manage, you owe your charges a good example to follow, truthful reporting, and thoughtful, hopeful planning. The alternative is oppression, and oppressors as well as oppressed fall before their time, taking everything they love down with them.

Points to Ponder

1. *Make a list of the expectations you had as you began your current position: which of them have come true? which have fallen short, or which have you seen exceeded? Why?*

2. *One of the great balancing acts in life occurs between self-interest and self-sacrifice. The ancients wrote a lot about self-sacrifice, while modern and contemporary writers tend to focus more on self-actualization, personal needs, desires, and achievements, the virtue of enlightened self-interest. Consider how you honestly feel about this question: is life more about individual survival and satisfaction, or more about the general good, be it of community, species, life, or planet?*

Conclusion

Beowulf and Your Career

If you read as I often do, you may have come directly to this final part of the book to get the main points and find out whether the whole of it deserves your time.

Or if you've diligently plowed through ideas, passages, applications, spotlights, and questions—thank you for your attention—you may need or want a summary of what the whole book means.

Let's view or review the major ideas we've covered, and then we'll finish by trying to estimate what good they offer you.

Beowulf is a profound, exciting epic poem about heroic adventures and the code of honorable behavior that those adventures exemplify and endorse. It traces the major martial deeds of a character, who in the poem is greatest man of his time, from his emergence as a hero to his death in a battle against a dragon. Beowulf the hero specializes in fighting monsters, undertaking tasks far too difficult for most human beings. He also becomes a successful king, ruling kindly and generously until his death. In addition to the main storyline, the poem also mentions and sketches out several other stories that the poet uses to expand on the ideas generated by the central plot. Those ideas, just as much as the story, live at the heart of the poem, which aims to explore and communicate the poet's understanding of life and success. We may employ them broadly; for instance, what *Beowulf* says about kingship we may interpret with respect to leadership more generally.

Beowulf taught its original audience about steadfast courage, generosity, honor, humility, leadership—in general about proper behavior for kings, queens, heroes, and anyone who aspires to noble deeds. The poem is unabashedly instructive.

The ancient tradition of books about how governors should govern and leaders should lead goes back at least as far as Plato and *The Republic*, and it shows no sign of slowing.

In addition to what we learn of medieval ideas of fame, praise, and glory—and the enjoyment we experience from a rousing adventure tale—*Beowulf* has a great deal to teach us that we can use in our own time, ideas that we can take with us into professional life about personal success as well as leadership. Each chapter of this book details a lesson directly from *Beowulf* and that idea's particular applications to contemporary life and work. We may summarize the most important ideas here.

Each of us must face up to mortality. If we learn how human beings have dealt with it in the past, we can better deal with it ourselves. If we learn how accepting mortality has helped them live better lives, we may learn ways to live better, more successful lives ourselves. We must realize that those who have trained us and prepared us for our own time in the spotlight will pass away, and we can't fully replace them. We can, though, appreciate and honor them, do our best, and fulfill our responsibilities to ourselves, our colleagues, and our families, and we can prepare the next generation with vigor and fervor equal to what the previous generation devoted to us. We must be willing to lead if the need falls to us, and when we lead we must unflinchingly accept responsibility for our own actions and for our followers' safety and progress.

We must prepare diligently for difficulty times that will inevitably come while living boldly and joyfully in the present, enjoying our talents and making the most of them: through them we find our greatest freedom and our greatest achievements. We must strive for a balance between an analytical focus and detail and the ability to look at problems and situations holistically. We may test our abilities and even brag about them, but we must be ready for the trials and back up the boasts.

When we set out to make peace, we must make peace, not try to embarrass the other side. When we travel abroad, we must fight the tendency to assume our own culture superior to theirs. In peace or war we must see every task through to its conclusion: try to ignore terror and it will find its way to your doorstep. We must live up to our responsibilities, commitments, and loyalties, but we must not sacrifice the principles of decency, compassion, and free will.

We should understand common notions of good manners and treat others respectfully, learning what we can of customs foreign to our own; we do well to balance cultural criticims and admiration for differences. We must understand both reason and emotion and allot them proper place in our experience. Showing emotion in appropriate contexts doesn't necessarily imply weakness; it may instead show one's own humanity.

We must allow the free play of ideas. We can always reject bad ones, but we must encourage the development of new ones. We will always have problems, old and new, to confront, and openness to new ideas balanced with reflection on old ideas will best help us solve them. Digressing from the expected course of thought or action may seem a waste of time, but it is often the only way to innovate.

We should value the arts of diplomacy and of speaking well and develop abilities in both. We must avoid romanticizing human nature or the nature of the world or of one or another culture. Keeping a sense of humor and irony helps, because we remain aware of the fact that people don't always act as we believe they should, and events don't always turn out as we hope or expect they will. Listening and learning without prejudice also help, because they permit us to see the good, absorb it, and act on it.

We may enjoy triumphs without blame, but we do well to avoid humiliating the defeated: the balance may soon change and our positions reverse. We should dare to be great, and we should dare to be kind.

That's a lot for one poem to say. The *Beowulf* poet didn't shy away from trying to share ideas.

Among the great works of the Old World, *Beowulf* serves up a particularly large number of quality nuggets of wisdom. Many other works also repay reading and study not just for their intrinsic value, but because we can apply what we learn from them to daily life. The faulty notion that only recent works have relevance to us encourages closed-mindedness in a time when our world is continuously shrinking and our knowledge is continuously growing, when we need more than ever to understand and evaluate the range of human experience. We need not love all we find, but we do need tolerance and understanding and the willingness to accept the fact that knowledge and useful wisdom may come from unexpected places—and times. In the Nineteenth Century Matthew Arnold called literature "the record of the best that's been thought and said in the world." New literature doesn't detract from or replace the old;

it adds to the tradition. Old and new alike may provide just the perceptions and insights we need to find keys to success: achievement, contribution, happiness. *Beowulf* offers a really good place to start.

*   *   *

The danger with career development is that you focus too exclusively on it, to the detriment of your personal life or to your responsibilities to the organization, or that you focus too little on it, whether from humility or timidity or lack of effort, and thus one way or the other you fail yourself. Your work does define a good deal of who you are to the world, though it need not limit how you develop or see yourself as a human being. Through your family, friends, community, or avocations you may find more joy and make greater contributions to the general good. But work takes up enough of your invaluable living time that you owe yourself and those who employ you a committed effort to do it well and to make your labor worth doing.

Productivity doesn't mean just the number of items you produce in a day or week or month. It implies also a dedication to quality, an understanding of the virtue of your labor and the value of your service, and a work ethic that drives you through from the beginning of a project to an end that you value. Nearly any task, anything from swabbing a floor to creating abstract art, has an intrinsic worth. You must look for the products and processes you value most and that, given your abilities, motivation, and energies, you can reasonably engage. A clean workplace, for instance, makes for a more pleasant environment in which everyone can be more productive, and art, real art of any sort, expands the mind into new regions of sensation, experience, creativity, sensitivity, and sensibility.

From *Beowulf* we learn that the world has always been tough: any given person, family, tribe, or culture has stood ever at the brink of destruction. Now, when we have marshaled such power that the whole world could tumble into chaos and darkness with the touch of a few buttons or with a few more short decades of neglect, we need as urgently as we ever have a better understanding of how to lead and how and whom to follow. We need heroic resistance against the monsters of bad ideas, destructive doctrines, and greed-mad regimes. We need even greater willingness to digress into new ideas, not to fall headlong into them, but to examine them for kernals of truth that will help us survive all the old and all the new problems.

We've suffered plenty of examples of bad leadership, of bad ways to run businesses and organizations and bad ways to treat our fellow creatures. We need to study new ways of producing and interacting, and we must commit ourselves to the virtues that make human life precious: freedom, equality, opportunity, careful and generous stewardship of resources, watchful vigilance, and the courage to respond against abuse, exploitation, and oppression.

Those are the global problems. On the personal scale, we all face the drive and need to live happy, satisfying, useful lives. That seems a simple goal, but the problems of the world have always made it difficult to accomplish.

The character Beowulf lives in a world with a firmly fixed set of values. Many of them, though not all, still have meaning for us today. While we no longer have a place for catastrophic blood-feud, we still need responsibility, fair play, good manners, willingness to learn and improve, adaptability, persistence, generosity, and sometimes tenacity and the willingness to see painful tasks through to the end.

We need to learn how to lead again. Leadership has always come first, I think, from charisma, but though charisma wins followers, it doesn't solve problems. Leaders need strategies, and they need compassion and magnanimity if their work is to produce any lasting results of value.

You and I will continue to struggle, sometimes enjoying, sometimes loathing our work, but with the process of building a career worthy of our energies. With the help of the great works of the greatest thinkers past and present, with our own ability to learn and shape our lives according to the values we most love and trust, and with a little luck we may not only make a living, but also, at least occasionally, accomplish something glorious.

Go get 'em.

About the Author

Edward Risden is currently Associate Professor of English at St. Norbert College in De Pere, Wisconsin. Originally from Ohio, he received his PhD from Purdue University in 1990.

He is currently working on a new novel and is looking forward to pursuing additional projects on the practical applications of classic literature like "Beowulf for Business." (Whitston has also published Ed's critically acclaimed "Beowulf in Faithful Verse.")

He has been teaching at the college level for more than twenty years and is a former president of the Medieval Association of the Midwest. He is the author of 10 books, and over 70 papers and articles in a variety of publications. This prolific literary output spans scholarship, criticism, fiction, poetry and drama.

His hobbies include cooking and practicing Tai Chi Chuan.

His wife, Kristy Deetz, is a painter and art professor at the University of Wisconsin in Green Bay.

Printed in the United States
78293LV00003B/181